THE CHEVALIER D'ÉON

Borgo Press Dramas by FRANK J. MORLOCK

The Chevalier d'Éon and Other Short Farces from the Eighteenth- and Nineteenth-Century French Theatre (Editor)
Chuzzlewit
Congreve's Comedy of Manners
Crime and Punishment
Falstaff (with William Shakespeare, John Dennis, and William Kendrick)
Fathers and Sons
The Idiot
Jurgen
Justine
Lord Jim
Notes from the Underground
Oblomov
Outrageous Women: Lady Macbeth and Other French Plays (editor and translator)
Peter and Alexis
The Princess Casamassima
A Raw Youth
The Stendhal Hamlet Scenarios and Other Shakespearean Shorts from the French (editor and translator)
The Widow's Husband; and, Porthos in Search of an Outfit: Two Dumasian Comedies (editor and translator)

THE CHEVALIER D'ÉON

AND OTHER SHORT FARCES
FROM THE EIGHTEENTH-
AND NINETEENTH-CENTURY
FRENCH THEATRE

FRANK J. MORLOCK,

EDITOR

THE BORGO PRESS
MMXII

THE CHEVALIER D'ÉON

Copyright © 2002, 2003, 2012 by Frank J. Morlock

FIRST EDITION

Published by Wildside Press LLC

www.wildsidebooks.com

DEDICATION

For Al Segal, my friend and doctor

NOTE

The Chevalier d'Éon was written by Charles Dupeuty (1798-1865) and Charles-Auguste Clever, Baron de Maldigny, and produced in 1837.

The Advantages of Being Ugly was written by Ernest Legouvé (1807-1903).

Colin and Colette was written by Pierre Beaumarchais (1732-1799).

Pregnant with Virtue (1783) and *Chaste Isabelle* (1720) were written by Thomas Guellette.

CONTENTS

THE CHEVALIER D'ÉON: A Play in Two Acts,
by Charles Dupeuty & The Baron de Maldigny . 9
CAST OF CHARACTERS. 11
ACT I. 13
ACT II 51
THE ADVANTAGES OF BEING UGLY, by
Ernest Legouvé 87
CAST OF CHARACTERS. 89
TEXT. 91
COLIN AND COLETTE, by Pierre
Beaumarchais 105
CAST OF CHARACTERS. 107
TEXT. 109
CHASTE ISABELLE: A PARADE, by Thomas
Gueullette 117
CAST OF CHARACTERS. 119
TEXT. 121

PREGNANT WITH VIRTUE, by Thomas
  Gueullette 135
CAST OF CHARACTERS 137
TEXT 139
ABOUT THE AUTHOR 155

THE CHEVALIER D'ÉON
A PLAY IN TWO ACTS
BY CHARLES DUPEUTY &
THE BARON DE MALDIGNY

CAST OF CHARACTERS

KING LOUIS XV

CHEVALIER D'ÉON

L'ABBÉ GRECOURT

MIGNONET, a locksmith

ZURICH, a Swiss concierge

SAINT-YVES, officer of the Royal Dragoons

THE MARQUISE DE POMPADOUR

MLLE BLANGY

OLIVE, the Chevalier's Valet

OFFICERS OF THE ROYAL DRAGOONS

LADIES OF THE COURT

SERVANTS

AN USHER

(eight men, two women)

ACT I

The stage represents a section of the Park at Versailles. To the audience's right, in the foreground, Zurich's cabaret. Nearby a grilled gate leading to the exterior of the park. To the left an arbor. In the back an enclosing wall.

AT RISE: Olive is on a horse by the wall at the back. The Chevalier appears without his sword, readjusting his uniform. His head is still covered, although inadvertently, with a lady's bonnet and wig.

OLIVE: (on horseback, by the wall) Where are you then, Chevalier? Are you lost in the bushes?

CHEVALIER: Here I am, here I am! (appearing behind the wall) Can I come down?

OLIVE: Yes, there's a trellis.

CHEVALIER: Help me a little. (Olive does) Good, good. I don't need you any more. Ah, there. Olive, are you quite sure that no one heard us flee, that no one saw us?

OLIVE: (on the wall) Perfectly sure, Chevalier.

CHEVALIER: (at the foot of the wall) Give me my sword.

OLIVE: (on the wall, handing it to him) Here! (during what follows Olive comes down stage)

CHEVALIER: (to himself as he attaches his sword to his belt) This darling Countess de Rochefort. I had only a minute before the arrival of her noble spouse to get out of my woman's dress and to jump over the wall decently. I couldn't show myself in the Park of Versailles in a silk dress and a ladies bonnet a la Pompadour.

OLIVE: (coming up, staring at him) Ah, my God, Mr. d'Éon. What forgetfulness.

CHEVALIER: What is it?

OLIVE: The bonnet, the lady's wig. It's all still there.

CHEVALIER: (taking off the bonnet) My word, that's true. It's all so light I didn't notice. (pointing to the bonnet) Sweet reminder of a charming rendezvous. Of my Jenny's crazy and coquettish hand. To satisfy a child's whim I adorned my head with this bonnet. How many beauties want one like this? As for me, I gave in. For in my adventures it's tit for tat to their husbands. It's well known I've given so many others finery.

OLIVE: Let's go back in, Chevalier.

CHEVALIER: You're right. This poor Countess Rochefort. So pretty, so lovable! We're not going to compromise her. It's enough to deceive her! She thinks I love her, that I adore her, while my heart belongs completely to my beautiful unknown. Come, let's prepare ourselves. For soon, here, it will be the hour of her mysterious promenades, under the somber alleys of this park.

OLIVE: Not to mention your welcoming luncheon that I've ordered at Zurich's.

CHEVALIER: If my unknown were to come during my absence. (they ring at the Park gate)

OLIVE: Hurry, hurry, Chevalier. I notice company already. I'm not mistaken. They are persons of the court and His Majesty, the King himself.

CHEVALIER: The King. And I promised the Minister of War not to dress as a woman any more! Let's escape, Olive, let's escape.

(They leave hurriedly. Zurich comes out of the cabaret and opens the gate. The King, Madame Pompadour, and Grecourt enter.)

POMPADOUR: Goodbye, Sire. Or rather till we see each other again. To accompany me almost to my carriage like a citizen of Paris escorting his wife to a carriage from Troyes! Do you know, Louis, that's a gallantry to which I am very sensible?

GRECOURT: (aside) She doesn't suspect a thing, poor woman.

KING: What, my beautiful Marquise, you persist in leaving Versailles to visit your aged uncle, The Commander?

POMPADOUR: I showed you the letter I received from his Steward. He's dangerously ill, this poor uncle, and he, who always served as a father to me; don't I at least owe it to him to close his eyes?

KING: You are an angel.

POMPADOUR: Besides, am I not confident of your love?

GRECOURT: (aside) Yes, count on that!

POMPADOUR: Something tells me that this trip will bring happiness to the good old man. He will be cured; I am sure of it. Especially as he's been abandoned by the doctors.

KING: Your sprightly wit will make him forget his sufferings. You will tell him all the spicy anecdotes of the court. That will remind him of his younger days. And in the evening to prepare him for sleep, you will read him some verses by this dear Grecourt.

GRECOURT: Sire, I am only too happy to lend myself to Your Majesty's laughter. (aside) You will pay me for it, despot.

KING: Wait, here's news in hand which will furnish you ample provision of scandal and excellent wickedness.

POMPADOUR: Ah, let's see, then. (reading) "Again, the Chevalier d'Éon," and further down "Again the Chevalier d'Éon". Why, it will still be the question of this inexplicable creature that everyone is talking about and that no one knows.

KING: The fact is it is an incomprehensible existence. (singing)

If you talk to old women
Who would completely damn their souls
To find a young swain again
They'd say, "She's a girl, for
Near us no fire lights up her eye.
And no one runs any danger
Beauties, beauties, scorn this frivolous creature.
Take our word; he's a chevalier
A chevalier deceitful and loose,
He makes you lose your head.

POMPADOUR: Why still, what is he then? (singing)

King, but speak to the young girls.
That one fine day he finds sweet
And that love knows how to catch
Shall say from the depths of her soul,
"Ah, despite his woman's clothes,
As for me, who shuns all danger
I want at least to protect you
Beauties, beauties, suspect this frivolous creature
For on my honor, he's truly
A chevalier, deceitful and loose."

POMPADOUR: (reading) "He makes you lose your head." See this article. "The old Marechale de Villars offers to bet that SHE left the convent. The young and pretty Countess de Rochefort assures that HE'S in the Musketeers."

GRECOURT: And as for me, I bet he's quite simply an intriguer or an adventuress.

KING: You are mistaken, Abbé, he's simply a scatterbrain.

MLLE DE BLANGY: (coming close) Is he a man?

KING: Yes, Miss. Our Civil Lieutenant took him to Tonnere and there on the register of the Parish he convinced himself that despite the whimsy of nature which has given him all the graces of a woman, our mysterious character is really the Chevalier d'Éon who's just purchased a company in the Royal Dragoons.

POMPADOUR: (aside to Mlle de Blangy) He's a he, I'm sure of it.

KING: Moreover, he promised on his honor to renounce for the future these disguises which could embroil him with Mr. D'Argenson.

A SERVANT: (entering) The Marquise's carriage is ready.

KING: Must you leave us?

MARQUISE: Not for long, I hope.

KING: The Trianon is going to be rather sad during your absence.

GRECOURT: (aside) She hasn't left yet.

KING: (singing)

Come back here soon.
My beautiful mistress.
For I cannot be happy
Far from your beautiful eyes.
Goodbye, my beautiful mistress
Goodbye, my love, goodbye!

(The King presses her to his heart and seems to say the most tender farewells.)

POMPADOUR: In this court that I am leaving, will

you remember me? Here love passes quickly. Even, alas, the love of a king. The love of a king is fleeting.

KING: (singing)

You alone reign over me.

GRECOURT: (aside) Oh, the Jesuit!

KING: Come back quickly, etc.

POMPADOUR: I leave and leave behind me all my tenderness! (singing)

Far from me, be happy.
Happy
For the two of us.
Goodbye!
All my tenderness
Goodbye.
You, my king, my God!

(The King leaves. Madame Pompadour is about to enter her carriage)

GRECOURT: (stopping her) Don't leave like this. And send your man away a bit.

POMPADOUR: (astonished) Why, for Heaven's sake?

GRECOURT: It's about your good and all your future.

POMPADOUR: Ah, my God, you terrify me. (she signals Mlle de Blangy and the servant to move away) Speak now, speak quickly.

GRECOURT: They are tricking you.

POMPADOUR: Who?

GRECOURT: The King.

POMPADOUR: Oh! That's impossible.

GRECOURT: Read this letter addressed to me which is signed by Lebel, the senior valet de chambre to the King.

POMPADOUR: (reading) "My dear Grecourt, you have your role in the conspiracy, you will equally have your reward. All is going well. The Marquise de Pompadour has been convinced that her uncle is dying and is going to put herself en route; and if our young novice subjugates the King, a nice exile will bring this proud favorite to reason. I shall have gold, the Duke de Stainville will be prime minister, and you, canon of one of our best vineyards." Oh, why this is frightful.

GRECOURT: Well, do you believe me now?

POMPADOUR: A conspiracy against me! And the King is in it! And I thought the king was so in love that I had the weakness of being faithful to him.

GRECOURT: You are departing from your character.

POMPADOUR: You don't know, Grecourt, in the long walks I take on foot, I love to play incognito along with my faithful Blangy. A charming young man attached himself to my steps; he spoke words of love to me, such as I'd never heard. And everything, even his name, engaged me not to discourage him. He's called the Chevalier d'Éon. Well, would you believe it, I had the cruelty to pain him, to repulse him, even to forbid him to try to see me again? Ah, if I had known.

GRECOURT: You will revenge yourself, right? You would have done as I am doing, if it must be confessed that if I come to you, if I've passed into the camp of the enemy it's because Louis XV has forced me to become a Coriolanus. Did you notice, even just now, how His Majesty lavished sarcasms, epigrams on me? Well, it's lasted now more than a week. He's made me the joke, the laughingstock of all these imbecile courtiers. Me! who never made anything but charming verses.

POMPADOUR: Oh, that's true! They're delicious. (aside) I've never read them but who cares?

GRECOURT: Fine. At least I've found someone who understands me. And a woman who understands them, a model of wit and learning. (aside) She doesn't know a word of French, but that always flatters.

POMPADOUR: United for vengeance.

GRECOURT: Poetic justice.

POMPADOUR: And a woman's revenge.

GRECOURT: The one is worth the other. But above all it's necessary to avoid the blow that threatens you. First of all, you know there's a huge party at the Trianon tonight?

POMPADOUR: And he said to me, "Trianon will be very sad during your absence": Oh, the traitor!

GRECOURT: The Great Masked Ball and the presentation of the young girl destined to dethrone you, Marquise.

POMPADOUR: Have you seen her? Is she pretty?

GRECOURT: Pretty as an angel.

POMPADOUR: Oh! I detest her.

GRECOURT: She's the daughter of an old employee, almost of the people, having the support only of her old mother, a poor widow that that scoundrel Lebel has deceived in the most unworthy manner. Her name is Marie Anna Dutertre, and she lives with her mother in the rue de Satory.

POMPADOUR: Little intriguer. I'm going to find her, overpower her with my wrath, and smash her. If need be, before the King himself.

GRECOURT: Giving all the more pretext for your exile. Stop. Don't do such a mad thing.

POMPADOUR: You are right. And I am conceiving a much better plan. First of all, I won't leave.

GRECOURT: It's not the moment.

POMPADOUR: You, you will work with my people who are devoted to me, and we will carry off my rival.

GRECOURT: Let's take her to Metz where she has some relatives. Admirable.

POMPADOUR: Hidden under this huge traveling cape no one will recognize me. I will reenter the Trianon; I myself will go to the rendezvous in place of Missing Beauty. And my royal traitor, confounded, stunned, will have no recourse but to fall at my knees and implore his pardon.

GRECOURT: Better and better. But I see two obstacles to that. First of all you cannot reenter the Trianon without being recognized for it's been forbidden to let anyone in, whoever they may be without an invitation from the Superintendent of Menus. And as for the mysterious pavilion of Rendezvous, you know the King alone has the key.

POMPADOUR: I had it before; prudently I made an impression. Find me a clever, discreet locksmith and this obstacle will be removed.

GRECOURT: I will find him for you.

POMPADOUR: As for the means to reenter the Trianon incognito, I'll think more of that later. But don't lose a minute.

MISS DE BLANGY: Marquise, your people will fear you've forgotten them.

POMPADOUR: They are going to receive my instructions. (to Grecourt) Go bring them, my friend. Yes, "my friend", I give you that title; the nine muses would be jealous of it.

GRECOURT: Ah! Majesty Louis XV, you intend to give a rival to the Marquise!

POMPADOUR: You find the witty Grecourt's verse bad!

GRECOURT: Well! We will see if you like the trick we are going to play you better! (aside) She is charming. (exit running)

POMPADOUR: He is charming!

MLLE DE BLANGY: What! Madame, you are not leaving?

POMPADOUR: No, my dear Louise, and you will

know why. (to herself) Ah! So they wanted to exile me, to make me abdicate, well, we shall see. What reassures me is that the King still loves me. Oh, yes. But for that would he fear to brave me face to face, or to indicate a polite dismissal? The King sees in this adventure only a fantasy to satisfy. Ah, Sire, you are providing me with a very bad example. (singing)

A really timid young officer.
Follows my steps everyday.
Timid from love you can't say.
Watching me with endless joy
When you turn your eyes away shyly
I resist as best I can.
But watch out!
He doesn't know I'm beautiful
He doesn't even know my name
Yet he loves me.
And as for me
Faithful up to now
I've always said no.
My beloved King.
God has protected you till now.
But watch out!
He's lovable, young, and in love
I'm resisting as best I can.
But watch out.

(speaking) My good Louise, what do you think of this young officer that we always meet on our solitary walks?

MLLE DE BLANGY: Oh, I find him charming, and it would truly have been a shame if he were to be a woman.

POMPADOUR: (writing on a paper that she tears out of a notebook) And do you think we will see him again today in this part of the park that he seems to like as we do?

MLLE DE BLANGY: Oh, I'd swear it. (voices arguing off) But what's that uproar?

POMPADOUR: Some officers heading this way. One would say a quarrel, a duel.

MLLE DE BLANGY: Let's escape, Madame. Let's get away.

POMPADOUR: No, stay. I recognized the uniform. (they lower their hoods and cling to the side behind the arbor)

D'ÉON: (entering first) It's no use going any further, gentlemen. (takes his sword in his hand and Saint Yves does as well)

MLLE DE BLANGY: It's him, Madame

POMPADOUR: Silence.

LAURAGUAIS: What are you thinking of, gentlemen? To draw your swords in the Park of Versailles, a few steps from the gate of Trianon!

D'ÉON: I won't have anyone mocking my love affairs, and especially the beautiful stranger.

MLLE DE BLANGY: (low) He's speaking of you.

POMPADOUR: Silence then.

SAINT YVES: As for me, I maintain she's old and ugly.

POMPADOUR: (aside) Insolent!

D'ÉON: I'm going to prove the contrary by giving you a little tap with the sword.

SAINT YVES: That's what we are going to see, by God.

(They go on guard and exchange several passes)

POMPADOUR: (coming forward) Stop, gentlemen, stop!

ALL: A woman!

D'ÉON: (aside) It's her.

POMPADOUR: I am the innocent cause of this duel.

I have the right to prevent two brave men from cutting each other's throat. Mr. de Saint Yves.

SAINT YVES: (aside) Heavens! She knows my name!

POMPADOUR: I cannot show you my face, but without failing in honor or truth, you can confess I am not old or ugly. (to d'Éon) You, Mr. d'Éon, Chevalier worthy of Amadis and handsome as Tristan. In the name of the lady of your thoughts, you are ordered to let your valiant swords rest. (they both sheath their swords.)

SAINT YVES: (aside) It seems to me I've heard that voice somewhere.

MLLE DE BLANGY: (low) Watch out! Mr. de Saint Yves is trying to recognize you.

POMPADOUR: Thanks for your gallantry, Vicomte. Chevalier, thank you for your obedience. Don't follow me; I forbid it. I beg you—

(She leaves quickly with Miss de Blangy but not before letting her bouquet fall at the feet of the Chevalier who was approaching her.)

D'ÉON: (watching her leave) Her bouquet! Oh, I will see her again. She loves me. Oh, yes, she loves me; it's impossible otherwise.

SAINT YVES: Happy mortal. You know, indeed, that now I would fight to be in your place. But at least you will tell us who this mysterious beauty is.

D'ÉON: Word of honor, I don't at all know. For a week I've seen her walk under the somber horse chestnut alleys. But she seemed to take care to hide her features from me and without having observed her face, without having seized a single glance from her, I became amorous—in confidence.

SAINT YVES: Amorous and brave! Oh! Now we have no further doubt.

D'ÉON: What do you mean?

SAINT YVES: You can grasp—we thought we were the butt of a joke by the Minister of War who sent us as a comrade, Amazon d'Éon. But you've proved your courage to us on the field, that you are a brave and true gentleman. Shake, Chevalier, and no hard feelings. (they shake hands)

ALL: Long live our new comrade.

D'ÉON: I hope to prove to you at my welcoming dinner that I don't recoil before Champagne any more than from a sword blow.

ZURICH: (with a thick German-Swiss accent) Herr offiziers, the repast is ready to be served.

SAINT YVES: Bravo, Zurich! (to d'Éon) Dear Amphitryon, we are all ready. We will drink to your amours, to your beautiful incognito.

D'ÉON: (aside) There's a letter in the bouquet. (quickly tearing it) I'm with you, dear comrades. Show me the way. Here, as in combat, I will always be with you.

ALL: To dinner! To dinner! (singing)

Dinner everybody!
Pop happy corks
May your noise answer
The sweet noise of song.

(They leave pall-mall. d'Éon pretends to follow them but returns on his tracks)

D'ÉON: A letter. I cannot resist my impatience. (reading) "We cannot tell you either her name or show you her face. But try to get yourself presented at court. As a sign of recognition she will carry a bouquet like the one she gave you." An unsigned letter, and no spelling errors; she's a great lady. Oh, I will see her again. I will recognize her. The residence of the King will be surrounded by a strict guard, but it's not impenetrable and the Supervisor of Menus cannot refuse me.

ZURICH: (who's just entered) Chevalier, sir. The company and the meal are waiting for you.

CHEVALIER: I'll be with them. Only ten minutes. (aside) Dear incognita, receive in advance all the kisses

I've given your letter. (kissing the letter and leaving hastily to the left)

ZURICH: Is he nuts? He kisses that paper as if it were covered with cutlets and gravy.

MIGNONET: (entering without seeing Zurich at first) A lady, a rendezvous with me, Mignonet the locksmith. That's more than singular! (noticing Zurich) Ah, it's you, my dear Uncle. Enchanted to see you, I wasn't looking for you.

ZURICH: Nephew, you are a clod.

MIGNONET: Papa Zurich, you are in error: you are my uncle on the maternal side, and I respect you infinitely, although you speak French badly.

ZURICH: How do you expect me to speak it? I dunno it.

MIGNONET: Ah! Barbarous Swiss! I dunno it. Why don't you speak carefully and with elegance. I cannot speak it, not knowing it. That's the way French is spoken.

ZURICH: (looking to his left) Ah, there's company cummin that way.

MIGNONET: (correcting him) Company coming.

ZURICH: Two girls.

MIGNONET: (aside) Ladies. That's my affair. (aloud) Papa Zurich, you are my uncle on my mother's side, and I respect you infinitely, but I have a false idea that they are calling you to go to the cellar.

ZURICH: To the cellar. I'm going. Goodbye, Mignonet (goes into the cabaret)

MIGNONET: Mignonet! I am masculine. What an obstinate fellow. If he should ever get to be a professor of grammar. (looking outside) Ah! The mysterious lady coming this way; she's seen me. She's told her servant to wait. What can she want with me? Doesn't Versailles know that I am engaged, almost married? It's a little bold on the part of this woman.

POMPADOUR: (aside) Ah, without doubt this is the workman Grecourt sent me.

MIGNONET: (aside) How she devours me with her eyes. Word of honor, it's indecent.

POMPADOUR: My friend.

MIGNONET: (aside) My friend! The effrontery, get out!

POMPADOUR: Didn't you come here on behalf of Mr. Grecourt?

MIGNONET: Yes, madame, yes, miss. I don't know exactly. But first of all, I must observe to you that the statement "my friend" is a bit free.

POMPADOUR: (aside) What's with this character?

MIGNONET: And that if you have given me this rendezvous to lead me into foolishness, it cannot be—

POMPADOUR: (aside) But he's made a mistake.

MIGNONET: I adore someone, and in plain French, I am quite determined not to commit any infidelity.

POMPADOUR: (aside) Ah, I understand.

MIGNONET: This someone is quite simply the prettiest girl in Versailles. Mr. Lebel, my client, the first valet de chambre to His Majesty told me "she's a morcel fit for a king".

POMPADOUR: (aside) Poor lad.

MIGNONET: Her name's Mary Anna Dutertre and everyone calls her Madame Mignonet.

POMPADOUR: The future wife of this little fellow; it's good to know.

MIGNONET: By an ingenuous diminutive I call her Nana, and as my name is Theodore, for her part, she's decorated me with the sobriquet Dodo.

POMPADOUR: (interrupting him) Relax, my boy. I

really hope never to be the rival of Miss Anna. But time presses, answer me.

MIGNONET: (aside) Heavens. That tone now! She's mortified.

POMPADOUR: You work with locks?

MIGNONET: Locksmith, at your service. (aside) It would appear it's not love, it's simply locksmithing. She's some big iron mongerer who wants to give me an order.

POMPADOUR: Could you make me a key I need in about two hours?

MIGNONET: In two hours! I will make you half a dozen. Do you want to come to the shop?

POMPADOUR: It's not necessary. Ten crowns will reward your work and your discretion.

MIGNONET: Ten crowns for a key! Ah, indeed. Do you want it in silver or gold?

POMPADOUR: (pulling out a folded paper from her notebook) There's an impression in there that will serve as your model.

MIGNONET: (aside) An impression. A false key, a confederate. Could she be a thief?

POMPADOUR: You feel you are paid too little? I will double the sum.

MIGNONET: Not at all, not at all, my beautiful lady. I don't eat that sort of bread; it's too hard for me. Ah, you take impressions and you want to make me an accomplice of picklocks? I'm going to call my uncle, the Swiss. I'm going to call everybody. And we'll see how you get out of that.

POMPADOUR: Stop! (aside) He's putting me in an embarrassing position. (as if struck by an idea) Ah, fortunately!

MIGNONET: What? Fortunately!

POMPADOUR: If gold makes no impression on you, there's another price which you won't be indifferent to.

MIGNONET: Yes, try a little.

POMPADOUR: Without knowing it, you've lost the most precious object.

MIGNONET: (fumbling in his pocket) You're mistaken. I haven't lost anything at all.

POMPADOUR: This very day your fiancée has been carried off.

MIGNONET: My Nana? Oh, no, no—that's not true, is it?

POMPADOUR: She's been carried off by Lebel—for the King.

MIGNONET: For the King! I am rather weak. (sits on a bench) (singing)

Seems to me I'm no longer the same man
And all things around me have changed.
Seems to me my dress of apple-green
'sbecome the shadow of sorrow.
But the pure shade of sorrow
A ridiculous, misshapen ornament
Comes over my face
And even my round hat
Changed its shape.

(spoken with rage) I am no longer astonished that scoundrel of a Lebel told me she's a morcel fit for a king. Horrible play on words.

POMPADOUR: Don't afflict yourself. I can return your fiancée to you.

MIGNONET: Return her to me without her having reigned a single day? (Pompadour makes an affirmative gesture) Oh, then you can count on me. I will make you keys, padlocks, safety locks, gates, bolts. I will beat down the filings for you.

POMPADOUR: Take this impression, and this evening, by means of a livery of the Château that Grecourt will procure for you, you will enter the Trianon and you will come find me. But with secrecy and without pronouncing my name.

MIGNONET: I believe so, indeed, since I don't know it.

POMPADOUR: You must at least be able to recognize my face.

MIGNONET: What do I see? The Marquise de Pompadour.

POMPADOUR: I hope that now you won't have any further doubt.

MIGNONET: The Marquise de Pompadour! The false Queen of France! And I who treated her like an iron monger.

POMPADOUR: In two hours, my key.

MIGNONET: And for me, my Nana. (sings)

Count on my zeal
I'm gonna be discreet.
I'm gonna be faithful
I want to see my girl again
Before tomorrow mornin'.

POMPADOUR: (singing)

I trust your zeal
You be discreet
You be faithful
And you'll be by your darlin'
Before tomorrow mornin'

MIGNONET: (aside and singing)

This secret key,
This lucky key
For Nana I am sure
Will get off scot free

(They take up the refrain together)

(Mignonet leaves)

POMPADOUR: I will have the key to the pavilion. But that's not all. How to get back into the Trianon while the King thinks I'm off to my uncle's château? All the fruit of my efforts would be ruined if I were to be recognized. I won't be able to surprise and confound my illustrious infidel. (considering) I can't see any way, and yet I must enter the ball. (looking outside) Ah, I see Grecourt. He will come to my assistance. But I'm not mistaken. He's not alone. Lebel, the first valet de chambre is with him. Will the Abbé after having betrayed the King to the favorite, have already betrayed the favorite to the King? These political abbes are subject to such rapid conversions. (she clings to the shadows to avoid being seen)

GRECOURT: (off) Yes, Mr. First, I understand perfectly what you are telling me.

POMPADOUR: (aside) They are separating.

GRECOURT: A great honor to see you again, estimable Mr. Lebel. (entering) The devil take you! Vile lackey, infamous sneak! I don't dare give him another name.

POMPADOUR: What's wrong, Grecourt?

GRECOURT: Wrong? I am ruined, lost, exposed to the wrath of the king.

POMPADOUR: What! Has our little kidnapping failed?

GRECOURT: No, it's not that. The little voyage is on its way and no one suspects the route she's taken.

POMPADOUR: Ah, I can breath. Now all that remains is for me to reenter the Trianon incognito. (she ponders)

GRECOURT: What do you mean all that remains? Well, and my adventure?

POMPADOUR: Ah, it's true. I'm no longer thinking. We'll speak of that later. (to herself) Yes, I will use—

GRECOURT: But I repeat to you, I am very exposed.

POMPADOUR: (without listening to him) No, that's not important.

GRECOURT: After the elopement, Mr. Lebel met me in the house and told me, positively, that if the young person is not found—

POMPADOUR: Well—

GRECOURT: It's certain everything will fall back on me. I will be arrested, imprisoned, beaten with sticks, perhaps.

POMPADOUR: (to herself) How lucky this is!

GRECOURT: What do you mean! Lucky that I will be beaten?

POMPADOUR: This is what I wanted.

GRECOURT: Madame, that's horrible ingratitude.

POMPADOUR: Eh! On the contrary, Abbé. It's a way of saving everything.

GRECOURT: I don't understand you.

POMPADOUR: You will have to find the little girl, whereas I must penetrate the château!

GRECOURT: Yes, but meanwhile, the green hood, the color of hope, the mask, everything is ready at the home of the beautiful fugitive.

POMPADOUR: Well?

GRECOURT: Lebel must come to find her within the hour, to lead her to the entrance to the Trianon, where the King will give her his hand.

POMPADOUR: Well?

GRECOURT: Well, I still do not understand you.

POMPADOUR: (aside) Still doesn't understand me? God, how stupid witty men are. (to Grecourt) The exact address of this family.

GRECOURT: (giving her a card) Here it is.

MLLE DE BLANGY: (entering) What does the Marquise wish?

POMPADOUR: Bring us a chair and a porter. (Miss de Blangy leaves. To Grecourt) Who will I find at this house?

GRECOURT: An old mother, too infirm to be able to follow her daughter. But who will be devoted to you. But if you would explain to me—

VOICES: (off) To the health of the Chevalier d'Éon.

POMPADOUR: The company at Zurich's! Happily my porters have come. (the porters enter with a chair) Goodbye, Abbé. We will see each other again at the Trianon. (gets into the chair)

GRECOURT: At the Trianon! I would still like to know—

POMPADOUR: (in the chair) Be very discreet! (to Porters) Rue Satory. (She closes the curtain and disappears)

GRECOURT: (alone) Be discreet! I think so! I don't understand. Favorite and King. Which of the two is the best? My, word, if I was asked: neither the one nor the other. Yes, still, whichever of the two will make me canon?

SEVERAL VOICES: (off) Another Champagne.

GRECOURT: Ah, here they are, the joyous companions who take their gambols to Zurich's cafe. That reminds me of my good times, when I had nothing, when I was only a vagabond poet.

MORE SHOUTS: Champagne! Champagne!

GRECOURT: Those shouts make me shiver. (singing)

How they howl
How often like men
I dressed casual for a happy party

That lasted till dawn
Long live the cabaret!
Fresh Claret wine
All is without affectation
When I drink
I'm king.
No one's above me.
Love reigns at court.
Imprisoned love
Love in a petticoat.
All falsely disguised.
As for me, I prefer
To live in dishabille
Long live the cabaret.
Kings are good sometime
When you flatter them
But Their Majesties
Do not always
Draw in their claws
Even with their loves.
Long live the cabaret.

(speaking) Ah, here are our gay guzzlers. They're leaving the table. Eh! By Jove, I'm not mistaken. They are acquaintances. The brave officers of the Royal Dragoons.

(Enter the Dragoons and d'Éon.)

CHORUS:

Great dining
That's the life
And we live today
Yes
For the one who invites
Doesn't know how to do things by half!

(they all shake Grecourt's hand)

SAINT YVES: Certainly, gentlemen, d'Éon's done things very well. The menu was excellent.

GRECOURT: And the wines?

SAINT YVES: Worthy of you, Abbé. But the Chevalier hasn't appeared at a dinner of which he's the Amphitryon. That's a bit much.

ALL: Here he is, here he is.

D'ÉON: (entering) Excuse me, my dear comrades for not arriving until the end of lunch; it's all the worse for me as I am dying of hunger.

GRECOURT: Well, let's start all over.

D'ÉON: Much obliged. When one is amorous the way I am.

GRECOURT: One doesn't eat. What a shame.

D'ÉON: Can you believe this Supervisor of Menus refused me an entry pass for the Trianon this evening under the pretext that one cannot go to court when one hasn't been there.

SAINT YVES: It's true. First you must be presented.

D'ÉON: He sent my request to the King, but the King knows my adventures, my pranks. I wouldn't even dare to be presented to him. And I had the nicest rendezvous. My friends, my comrades, help me, show me a way. Whoever can open the gates of this abode for me, I will cede to him the love of three countesses, the letters of a Marquise and a lock of La Guimard's hair.

GRECOURT: Indeed, I have an entry pass.

D'ÉON: Really?

GRECOURT: But it's a pass for a woman.

D'ÉON: May the Devil take you!

GRECOURT: It's for Baroness de Fromonville, my relative, who was to make her first appearance today at court but who had the stupidity to sprain her ankle recently at a ball. (drum roll off)

D'ÉON: What's that noise?

GRECOURT: It announces the arrival of the king to us shortly.

D'ÉON: And I cannot enter! What will she say of me, of my blunder?

GRECOURT: I'll concern myself with it; I will speak to the King.

CHORUS:

Did you hear the sequel to the ball?
The mysterious veil authorizes love and pleasure.
In this royal abode
Everything speaks to us of love
Dancers, frolicsome maskers rush about.

POMPADOUR: (raising her mask and showing her face to Grecourt) Now do you understand?

GRECOURT: (aside) The Marquise.

POMPADOUR: (seeing d'Éon) He's here!

D'ÉON: (aside) The same bouquet at her side. It's she and with the King. What mystery.

KING: (to the Marquise at the left of the stage) Beautiful Marie, are you going to persist in this obstinate silence? You know you are without rivals?

POMPADOUR: (changing her voice) Except for Madame Pompadour.

KING: That poor Marquise, she's traveling at the

moment and doesn't suspect a thing.

POMPADOUR: I pity her with all my heart.

D'ÉON: (pulling Grecourt by his cloak) Speak then!

GRECOURT: I'm getting ready. (aloud) Sire—

KING: What do you want, Abbé?

GRECOURT: The Supervisor of Menus sent a personal decision to Your Majesty regarding the admission of young Chevalier d'Éon to this party and I dare hope—

KING: (interrupting him) The Chevalier d'Éon—that bad actor—

GRECOURT: I'm not saying otherwise.

D'ÉON: (aside) Thanks. (pinches Grecourt)

KING: Let him beware of ever presenting himself to us. Instead of an invitation to a ball he runs a great risk of receiving a letter of imprisonment.

D'ÉON: (aside) Tyrant, go away.

POMPADOUR: (low to Chevalier and very quickly) Find a way. I wish it.

D'ÉON: (aside) She wishes it. (to Grecourt) Abbé, do you promise to second me?

GRECOURT: With all my power.

D'ÉON: Well then, I will go to this ball.

KING: (to the Marquise) So stingy with words? Will you be the same with this pretty hand?

(The Marquise abandons her hand to him, which he kisses.)

KING: (aside) this simple favor transports me, intoxicates me. And yet it's only a variation. (aloud) I've made a new conquest. I haven't wasted my day.

POMPADOUR: Sire, the day doesn't end until midnight.

D'ÉON: (low to the Marquise) At the Trianon.

CHORUS: Do you hear the signal for the ball? The veil of mystery, etc.

(The King gives his hand to Madame de Pompadour, and preceded by the dancers goes toward the gate of the Trianon. Grecourt, d'Éon, and the officers, consult together.)

CURTAIN

ACT II

The stage represents a rich, octagonal pavillion. Doors on the sides. At the back a door giving on an illuminated garden. To the left a table with ink, feather pens, paper. Chairs, arm chairs. Candelabras with lighted candles.

POMPADOUR: You also got into the Trianon to join me, my dear Blangy?

MLLE DE BLANGY: When you have two big black eyes and a young page notices them—

POMPADOUR: I understand. Two beautiful eyes open all doors more readily than one golden key. But on the subject of the key, that young worker's really making me wait, and that begins to worry me. Because I cannot get into my apartments except through the secret door that gives on this pavilion. Meanwhile, as the King was speaking to Mr. de Berries about I don't know what plan to marry the Prince de Condé, I softly disengaged my arm from his and escaped. But if they find the green hood, everything will be ruined.

MLLE DE BLANGY: Madame, here's a servant in the livery of the château who seems to be looking for someone.

POMPADOUR: It's him.

MIGNONET: (entering in a livery that is much too large) I'm not mistaken. It's my pretty lady from before.

POMPADOUR: Yes, my friend.

MIGNONET: I recognized you right away despite the strange costume. This becomes you much better. I pay you my compliment. Permit me to say to you that I think you are a very beautiful woman.

POMPADOUR: (smiling) Really, my friend?

MIGNONET: A very beautiful woman.

POMPADOUR: Even from a workman that's pleasing.

MIGNONET: As for me, it's different. I won't say anything of my new clothes. The badges of domestic service are repugnant to me. And this outfit doesn't fit me at all.

POMPADOUR: Indeed, I beg you—

MIGNONET: (giving her a key) Here's the object.

POMPADOUR: (to Miss Blangy) Try this key.

MLLE DE BLANGY: Yes, Madame.

MIGNONET: That ought to open to the left.

MLLE DE BLANGY: (opening the door) Yes, and perfectly.

MIGNONET: To speak plainly, I dare to think that's because the work was well done.

POMPADOUR: Give your purse to this man.

MIGNONET: (aside) Some gold coins she's holding there! (aloud) Thanks, thanks, Marquise. But there's yet another thing to return to me.

POMPADOUR: What's that?

MIGNONET: My Nana.

POMPADOUR: Ah, yes! I wasn't thinking of it any more.

MIGNONET: Well, as for me, I'm thinking about it. I think about it constantly, and the more I do, the more horrible suspicions I have that she is here.

POMPADOUR: In the Trianon?

MIGNONET: In this Trianon.

POMPADOUR: Oh, relax. I tell you she's not here.

MIGNONET: Because I overheard a conversation at a banquet. "Yes," said Mr. Lebel, my infamous character, "they wanted to take her away from us, but she's been found again."

POMPADOUR: (laughing) Oh, I divine who's deceived you. (in a serious tone) But, if they've deceived me—

MIGNONET: Yes, if they've deceived you.

POMPADOUR: Oh! Thanks to this lucky key I will soon clear everything up.

MIGNONET: Oh, yes, soon, I entreat you. Before my future wife has had the honor of seeing His Majesty. I prefer she be returned before rather than after.

POMPADOUR: Go, go, my friend, and rely on me.

MIGNONET: Yes, yes, Madame. I have the greatest confidence, I beg you. (aside) God! If she were to forget me. If Nana was weak enough to accept a rendezvous in this devilish pavilion. Fortunately, I have taken my precaution. (to Pompadour who is looking at him) I'm going away, I'm going away, Marquise. But I entreat you: soon as possible, as soon as possible. (he leaves)

POMPADOUR: Was this lad right? And has Lebel been able to track down this young girl? Bad luck to her if she has had the audacity to get in here, and to aspire to replace me. Even for a day. I am jealous, and jealous for the love of a King. (bursts of laughter and bravos outside) Now what's that uproar?

MLLE DE BLANGY: Young lords and ladies of the court who are wandering laughing through these illuminated gardens. Ah, I notice, also, the uniform of the regiment of your young and gallant chevalier.

POMPADOUR: He is here; that's a proof of love. Whereas, Louis—! Beware, Louis of France, King though you be. Misfortune could come to you.

MLLE DE BLANGY: What misfortune?

POMPADOUR: He's forgotten that my name is Madame Pompadour. (as they leave by the right the officers, Saint Yves, Lauraguais and The Chevalier in drag enter.)

CHORUS:

On the King's behalf
Make all ready
So pleasure reigns
In his name
Happy dancers
It's a big party
It's a big party
At the Trianon.

SAINT YVES: Room! Room! I announce to you

the new beauty presented at court today: Baroness Fromonville. (The Chevalier enters, a little Negro carries the train of his dress)

THE LADIES: She's charming.

CHEVALIER D'ÉON: Ah, ladies. (he curtsies)

MEN: Greetings to the Queen of the Ball.

D'ÉON: Ah, gentlemen. You make me blush.

A LADY: I am somewhat related to the Fromonville's. Will you give me a hug, my dear? (she embraces him)

D'ÉON: With great pleasure, my dear relative. (aside) This is beginning very well.

LAURAGUAIS: Miss—would I be lucky enough to dance a minuet with you?

D'ÉON: (curtsying) With great pleasure, Count. (changing tone) But no more jokes. Tell me, have you been luckier than I? Have you noticed in the midst of these thousand beauties who are present at the party, a lady with a fanciful bouquet with flowers like these?

ALL: My word, no.

D'ÉON: Then they will be mocking me, that's certain. And I will be out the cost of my disguise.

SAINT YVES: Of what do you complain? Haven't you made enough conquests? Just now in the arms of Grecourt, Brissac, Gisors. Even the Duke de Richlieu made you his declaration. What an honor for the regiment.

D'ÉON: But did you notice that Lebel, The King's First Valet de Chambre was observing me, following me all the time? If he should suspect something?

SAINT YVES: Oh, then watch out, my poor d'Éon.

D'ÉON: Oh, no matter. I must find her again.

SAINT YVES: Silence. They're listening to us.

D'ÉON: In truth! Gentlemen, you are not gallant. I cannot dance with everybody. Mr. Lauraguais, you offered me your hand first and I accept it.

ALL: But we have written our names and we won't suffer it.

D'ÉON: Ah, mercy gentlemen. A little indulgence for the ladies, no scenes, no quarrels. Spare my poor nerves, I am so delicate, so timid. (giving his hand to Lauraguais, and making a deep curtsy.) Gentlemen, I know you. (with a man's voice) Ah, by God, if they are making fun of you we will see who has the last laugh. (leaving with Lauraguais.)

SAINT YVES: Word of honor, the cleverest get caught,

and we are lucky to be in on the secret. Why, here's the joyous Grecourt. (enter Grecourt) Eh! Come over here, dear Abbé, so we can pay you a compliment. You had the most clever idea.

GRECOURT: Yes, an idea that may get us all condemned to the Bastille.

ALL: To the Bastille?

SAINT YVES: What's going on?

GRECOURT: Wait while I calm down, for I am still beside myself. By such a freak of nature. First of all, it seems, it's even certain, that a young girl, the beauty in the green domino, succeeded in escaping even though she was on the arm of the King.

SAINT YVES: But what connection can that have?

GRECOURT: Wait. Soon consoled for this loss, Louis XV put himself to wandering through the Ball. At that moment, I gave him the arm of d'Éon, that of our counterfeit Baroness.

SAINT YVES: And His Majesty has discovered everything, guessed all?

GRECOURT: (grouping them around him) Listen, the secret is the more inconceivable, the more shocking. His Majesty, The King himself, is smitten with a sudden passion.

SAINT YVES: What Louis XV?

GRECOURT: Hush! It's as I have the honor of telling you. I am still trembling in all my parts. Lebel, the infamous Lebel, came to accost me. "Grecourt," he said to me, "The King has noticed Miss de Fromonville and he charges you to ask on his behalf, a moment's conversation with your protege." At these words I felt myself stupefied, without strength, as if I hadn't drunk water for two weeks, and I came to find you, you my accomplices, my friends, to save me from this frightful position.

SAINT YVES: My word, dear Abbé, we know, word of a gentleman, how to draw the sword or undo the cords of a purse, you can count on us. But the Bastille! No women, no air! no delightful meals. Nice seeing you! We are vanquished. The battle is lost. Save yourself if you can.

ALL: Save yourself if you can. (They leave running)

GRECOURT: (alone, running after them) Gentlemen, my friends, I entreat you. Bah! I can no longer see them. They are already saying that the Police Lieutenant is at their heels. Well, am I in a fix! They are leaving me in a pretty pickle. I've still got to leave at any cost, for I don't want the Bastille any more than they do. There's no time to lose. Soon this pavilion, open to all to avoid suspicion will become a retreat where light and darkness obey the will of a master as in a fairy palace. If the King were to find me there instead of the beauty he came looking for, he's the man to kill me on the spot. What to do? My God, what to do? (reflecting) These officers and gentlemen have left all the responsibility on me. If I were to deliver myself of this burden in my turn, if I changed it to one of them, yes, that would be fair play. I observe d'Éon. Let's try.

D'ÉON: (entering in the greatest agitation, walking in like a man, followed by his Negro who still holds the train of his dress) I am furious. There's not a bouquet in this ball that resembles mine. It was a hoax. I can no longer doubt it, and I'm enraged. (he commences to march back and forth, kicking the Negro) Get out! You! You annoy me! (the Negro runs away)

GRECOURT: Why, Chevalier, you are not thinking. A girl of quality never walked in this manner. You are going to betray yourself.

D'ÉON: Perfidious!

GRECOURT: My friend—

D'ÉON: Leave me alone. It's you who put me up to this folly.

GRECOURT: Look, calm down. Perhaps you haven't as much to complain of as you think.

D'ÉON: Huh! What are you saying?

GRECOURT: A young lady—

D'ÉON: And beautiful—

GRECOURT: And beautiful—is present like you at this celebration. You know it.

D'ÉON: Doesn't she, in her turn, have a bouquet like mine?

GRECOURT: Yes, yes, very like. (aside) I don't know what he means, but it's all the same.

D'ÉON: And she consents to see me?

GRECOURT: She herself demands it.

D'ÉON: Ah, my friend, my dear friend, how nice you were to have found a way for me to enter the Trianon! Where will I see her?

GRECOURT: Right here.

D'ÉON: Where?

GRECOURT: Soon.

D'ÉON: Oh. Right away. But I wonder why, up to now, has she been so cruel as to avoid me?

GRECOURT: She accuses you of having deceived, abused her.

D'ÉON: Why, that's a slander.

GRECOURT: Exactly. Rumors that slander have been spread about you. She's—she's harbored them. They told her, they affirmed that the handsome captain of the dragoons was only a bold and wicked girl, playing at seducing, under the clothes of a man and then delivering the women who were weak enough or romantic enough to listen—to the laughter of the public.

D'ÉON: (gaily) What! Is that all it is?

GRECOURT: And it's to overwhelm you with reproaches that she insists on an interview with you.

D'ÉON: To believe me a woman! Oh! I will justify myself. You told me she'd be here in an instant; thanks, my friend, my dear friend, I will never forget such a service.

GRECOURT: It's truly nothing. (shaking his hand) Courage and eloquence!

D'ÉON: Oh. I won't lack it.

GRECOURT: (aside) My, word, Mr. d'Éon. Get yourself out of this if you can. And in my turn, save yourself if you can. (he leaves)

D'ÉON: (alone) Then I'm going to know my unknown. Eh, why I've never looked this pavilion over so carefully. What luxury. Why, this is a royal apartment.

Everywhere, the doors in crimson velour. And the cipher of Louis XV—interlaced. Is it possible I am in the home of a princess? (the door at the back locks) What! They're locking me in? It seems that beauty doesn't want me to escape her. The candles no longer give anything but a weak light. Is everything done here by magic? Ah! My God! I heard a door open, and something that resembles the brushing of a dress. How my heart beats. (he leans on an armchair)

POMPADOUR: (entering from the right, aside) A woman! Ah! I suspected in the transports of my jealousy that man was right. Louis must have found his new conquest. Well, so much the worse for her.

D'ÉON: (aside) She doesn't dare speak to me, address me. Come, it's up to me to take the first step.

POMPADOUR: Little wretch! (giving d'Éon a vigorous smack)

D'ÉON: Ah! For goodness sake, that's a bit much. Is it for this you gave me a rendezvous?

POMPADOUR: Me! A rendezvous to a woman of your sort?

D'ÉON: Yes, Madame, a rendezvous.

POMPADOUR: What a voice! Leave, insolent one, or I will no longer be able to answer for my rage.

D'ÉON: Well, no, Madame! I won't leave. I won't leave before having justified myself.

POMPADOUR: You intend to justify such infamous conduct?

D'ÉON: I know you think ill of me, but at least you should hear me before treating a gallant man this way.

POMPADOUR: (astonished) A gallant man! What's she saying?

D'ÉON: Oh, Madame, I know that word astonishes you, perhaps, enrages you. But I have to destroy the terrible slander that they've uttered to you on my account. To say that I am a woman, a schemer, whoever dares to maintain that, I will put my saber through his body.

POMPADOUR: What! nonsense! Mademoiselle, aren't you a young girl whose ambition has led you to be seduced by the snares of that infamous, Lebel?

D'ÉON: On my honor, I am the Chevalier d'Éon.

POMPADOUR: (aside) The Chevalier having a tete a tete with me, and brought about by the King!

D'ÉON: They gave me a name, the clothes of a woman, and I took it all without asking questions, to see the one I love, the one I will love forever. (wanting to go to her)

POMPADOUR: Oh, Chevalier, you are an infidel. And

if your unknown heard you—

D'ÉON: Oh! My unknown cannot be anyone except you. You to whom I vow my life; you to whom I prefer no other woman, were she the Marquise de Pompadour.

POMPADOUR: And if the Marquise and your unknown were the same woman?

D'ÉON: Oh, then I would throw myself at her feet, and I would never leave that entreating posture until I heard my pardon from her mouth.

POMPADOUR: Get up Miss, you are going to damage your dress. Oh, all this is Grecourt's scheme, I divine it, and it can be useful to my plans.

D'ÉON: Oh, my God. I heard some noise.

POMPADOUR: No, no. You're mistaken. Don't be afraid.

D'ÉON: It's not for myself. But if they surprised us. You so good, so indulgent, at night with a young man.

POMPADOUR: Poor lad! And I gave you such a smack! (singing)

To punish myself for that sin
I have to commit another
And give you the hand
That struck you!

(offering him her hand)
D'ÉON: (kissing her hand) See. I bear no grudge.
POMPADOUR: (aside/singing)
Louis, my King
This is your doing
Let's obey
Your absolute power.

D'ÉON:

But a smack
Is a terrible affront.

POMPADOUR: How to be forgiven?

D'ÉON:

If you made my cheek blush
Let your lips
Cover it with rouge.

(D'Éon leans down and Pompadour kisses his face)

POMPADOUR: (refrain)

Louis my King
This is your doing
Let's obey
Your absolute power.

D'ÉON: This time, I'm not mistaken. I heard someone walking outside.

POMPADOUR: Don't be worried about me. Don't I have this key which opens both doors, and this third, which leads to my apartments?

D'ÉON: (excitedly) Let's both escape that way.

POMPADOUR: No, it's necessary for me to remain here. I need this proof. (aside) Ah, King Louis of France, we shall see. (aloud) Whatever happens, don't be astonished. Don't be frightened by anything. And count on me, my sweet Chevalier. (she leaves rapidly by the door to the right and locks it. As the Marquise leaves, night comes on.)

D'ÉON: (at the door she just left) Au revoir, my beautiful Marquise. They are opening the door at the back. Come. I am having adventures here.

MIGNONET: (at back) The Marquise has forgotten me; I was sure of it; but she doesn't suspect I kept a key for myself.

D'ÉON: (aside) It's a man's voice.

MIGNONET: (aside) And that I can solve this horrifying mystery myself.

D'ÉON: (aside) What's he come here to do?

MIGNONET: If she's really in the château, it's here she must be locked in.

D'ÉON: (aside) Perhaps he's a rival. I'm unarmed.

MIGNONET: (aside) It seems to me I saw something move down there in the corner. (aloud, calling) Miss Nana.

D'ÉON: Who's there?

MIGNONET: (aside) She answered. She's here.

D'ÉON: Once again. Who is there?

MIGNONET: (aside) How her voice has changed! Perhaps she's taken cold. Come, come. Some nerve, and cover her with shame. (aloud) You ask who's there, fickle Nana?

D'ÉON: (aside) Nana?

MIGNONET: You pretend not to recognize me, hussy!

D'ÉON: (aside) Ah! Indeed! What's this bully want with me?

MIGNONET: I, Theodore Mignonet, locksmith by trade, infatuated by your attractions—through stupidity—

D'ÉON: (aside) He's a madman escaped from the loony bin.

MIGNONET: (groping his way, peering) Ah! It won't

do you any good to keep quiet. You won't escape me, slut! I will save you from the abyss and you will follow me to the home of your respectable mother.

D'ÉON: (disengaging, abruptly) Will you release me, animal?

MIGNONET: Ah! Animal! You push me away, once, twice, three times. Are you going to follow me? Follow me, I advise you or I'll get carried away. I am striking without seeing clearly. (raising his hand)

D'ÉON: Ah! This time, by Heaven, you won't be the first to strike. (whacks him)

MIGNONET: God! What a clout! (singing)

I've seen three million stars.

D'ÉON: (Singing)

Ah, rogue. That'll teach you to
Respect the ladies.

MIGNONET: (singing aside) If the adventure begins this way Ah, I feel that she could hurt me.

D'ÉON: (singing aside)

My word, I can't understand it.
But this gift I was given
Weighs on my conscience

And I need to return it.

MIGNONET: Why this is a horror, an infamy, a vile deed. I am going to shout thief, fire, murderer!

D'ÉON: Hell and Damnation! If you say a single word—

MIGNONET: (aside) Great. Now she's swearing. (aloud) Nana.

D'ÉON: Nana. He's at it again.

MIGNONET: Come to yourself, and despite the darkness, recognize the cherished features that conquered you. Recognize your Dodore. (at this moment the candles spontaneously light up) Gods! What blinding light. (rubbing his cheek) Did I already receive something?

D'ÉON: (aside) What's this mean? Would it be the beginning of the test? I absolutely must send this imbecile away.

MIGNONET: I hope that now, in broad daylight, you will no longer dare to deny. Heavens, it's not Nana! (he runs out locking the door behind him)

D'ÉON: (alone) He spared me the trouble of putting him out the door. With all that, here I am, alone in the midst of an intrigue in which I am the actor without anyone having taken me in their confidence. My word,

I will see it through to the end. (sings)

The mistress who reigns here
Loves me.
Yes, it's no dream!
I am still heedless
Of the rank to which her love raises me
She's already allowed me
To usurp His Majesty's power
With a further proof of her bounty
And I am almost King of France.

(speaking) But it seems to me they've left me prisoner a long time. With that, I feel in the pit of my stomach, like a pressure—Maybe it's my corset that's making me feel ill. No, it's that I'm hungry, very hungry, and very thirsty. With all these adventures it's been twenty-four hours that I've forgotten to take something. Modestly, a true lover ought not to ask to eat. It's too prosaic. But my darling Marquise still would have been able to think of me. (at this moment, a trap opens and an elegant laid out table with two place settings appears on stage) Ah, my God, am I awake? What! served on wish. Why, this is fairy like. My word, fairy or not I'm going to risk myself. I am curious to see if the supper is enchanted. (sits and eats and drinks avidly) No, this is really an excellent pate. Let's see the wine! (pours out a big glass) Perfect, perfect. You couldn't drink any better in my dear village of Tonnere. But I notice there are two place settings. And here I am, I didn't wait. How impolite that is. It's doubtless the tete a tete supper that my beautiful friend arranged for me. What a lovely surprise. But since all come here at will, without doubt, the beneficent fairy won't need to be prayed for more. (aloud) Enchantress I evoke you.

(The door to the left opens and the King appears. The orchestra plays God Save the King.)

D'ÉON: (noticing him) The King! I am lost. (rising with the greatest embarrassment and wiping his mouth with his napkin)

KING: (smiling) Don't disturb yourself my proud beauty.

D'ÉON: Oh, Sire. I swear to you I'm not hungry. I haven't the least appetite.

KING: What would she do when she is? It seems she's a bouncing wench. She swallows a glass of Burgundy easily enough.

D'ÉON: (aside) I can see by his ironic smile he knows my folly and my disguise will cost me dear.

KING: Come, compose yourself, charming Fromonville.

D'ÉON: His Majesty's making fun of me.

KING: Lebel warned me that you have a lively and provincial frankness. And that there is not in my court any woman like you.

D'ÉON: Sire, he told you the truth. (aside) I must confess everything. That's the easiest way.

KING: As to the rest, it's my fault, my little baroness, if I find you dining. I made you wait a bit. Can you imagine, I stopped to laugh for a moment at what happened to that poor, poor wife of Marshall Villeroi; a young woman dressed like a man—

D'ÉON: (aside) Ah! My God!

KING: Very smitten of her husband; she was introduced to his hotel and seduced the tender Marechale. Can you conceive anyone being so deceived by a transvestite?

D'ÉON: No, no. I cannot imagine it at all.

KING: I would never let myself be amused to such a degree.

D'ÉON: Oh, no, for goodness sake. (aside) I don't dare say any more to him.

KING: Moreover, if I had so little wit to allow myself to be taken in, the Bastille is too discreet to allow anyone to laugh at my experience.

D'ÉON: (aside) I'm more dead than alive.

KING: But let's only speak of you, my proud beauty and learn the motive why I had you come to this rendezvous.

D'ÉON: I don't feel myself at ease. I wish to withdraw.

KING: Oh, I am too gallant to suffer it. You know that from the example of my ancestor, Louis XIV, who deigned to dance in the ballets of Moliere, I have resolved to try a step in the party we are giving tonight at the Trianon.

D'ÉON: Yes, Sire and it even seems to me that you ought to dance that step with the Marquise de Pompadour.

KING: Mustn't be jealous.

D'ÉON: Jealous!

(sings)

Lots of ladies
I know
Have a lech for you
Love for the Prince, The King
But as for her
It's the man she loves.

KING: (sings)

By my faith
You defend her

With a concern, a zeal

D'ÉON: (sings)

Because despite that
No one knows better than I
How faithful she is to you.

KING: It's possible. It's very generous on your part. Nevertheless it won't be the Marquise who dances tonight with the King.

D'ÉON: But who then?

KING: You, my pretty, pretty.

D'ÉON: Me, Sire? But I don't know how to dance.

KING: It's a school girl's trick. Besides, we are going to try it, to rehearse a little. (dance music is heard) Wait, do you hear? Place yourself there. You will be the pupil. And I will be the dancing master.

D'ÉON: (aside) And as for me that only remembers the school of a cavalry man, feet lightly in the stirrups—

(The King places his sword on an armchair to the right)

KING: Are you ready?

D'ÉON: But Sire, I repeat to you, I don't know how to dance at all.

KING: Come on. I don't wish to provoke you, but at least you cannot refuse me what you have so well begun. (offering her his hand, pointing to the table)

D'ÉON: (sitting) Willingly, Sire.

KING: (aside) She's truly original. (pouring wine) To you, Baroness, the honor of the first toast.

D'ÉON: To the health of the noble King of France, to his military department, the French guards, and his fine regiment of Royal Dragoons.

KING: (aside) Now that's a singular toast for a lady. (drinks) (aloud) My turn, pour my dear Hebe. (aside) Our prudes at the court will be jealous of my new conquest. So much the better. (coming forward to the left at the same time Madame Pompadour enters from the right; she makes a sign for d'Éon to shut up) To the health of she who is most dear to me, the lady of my thoughts. (turning he finds himself with Madame Pompadour who has silently taken the cup from the Chevalier) Marquise!

POMPADOUR: To the health of the most faithful of lovers.

(The King places his cup on the table; the Marquise hands hers to the Chevalier who gulps it down)

KING: You here, Madame! I thought you were with

your sick uncle.

POMPADOUR: My uncle is doing marvelously, Sire.

KING: And, instead of leaving, you dared to return incognito to Trianon?

POMPADOUR: I am much too good a subject to allow myself to refuse the hand His Majesty offered me with so much grace.

KING: (aside) It was she! (aloud) And without doubt we offered you the hand to penetrate this pavilion where none can enter without our order.

POMPADOUR: Your Majesty is forgetting that he gave me the key.

KING: You have a memory, Marquise. Well, you must remember that you possess a very beautiful château at Etioles.

POMPADOUR: Whose air would be very good for my health, right?

KING: You've understood me. I don't like anyone braving me. And henceforth—(noise of confusion outside) What's that noise?

VOICES OUTSIDE: Attention! Attention! To arms!

POMPADOUR: Ah, My God! Could that be a revolt?

Ah, Sire, at the moment of danger you aren't going to thrust me from your arms.

D'ÉON: Is the life of the King threatened? (grasping the King's sword and brandishing it expertly) True God, Let them come.

KING: (with admiration) What a woman!

VOICES OUTSIDE: Stop! Stop that fury!

D'ÉON: Sire, I will place myself on guard at your door, and were there ten thousand of them I will have their heads; I swear it by the flag of my regiment.

(The noises stop)

POMPADOUR: (aside) He's giving himself away.

KING: What, Miss! Your regiment? (leading him quickly downstage.)

D'ÉON: (aside) I'm caught.

KING: Explain yourself, explain yourself. I wish it.

D'ÉON: (singing)

To enter this circle
I had recourse to a trick
But, Sire, they are threatening your life.
No more tricks, no more disguises

Yes, from this moment the error ceases.
And you see, I confess,
Under this furbelow, linen
A Captain of the guards.

POMPADOUR: (pretending surprise) What, Sire! A young man and so close to my apartment? Just see what you were exposing me to.

KING: Silence, Madame. And you, sir. Your name?

D'ÉON: The Chevalier d'Éon.

KING: What! That bold young man who has already mocked with his transvestite apparel so many wives and husbands. Sir, you will learn one does not mock me with impunity.

D'ÉON: Sire, I only had such audacity to see the one I love. The one I will love all my life. I've seen her; she spoke to me.

KING: Well, that's a happiness that I won't refuse you. (writing) I am going to commend you to the Minister of War, and especially to the Governor of the Bastille.

POMPADOUR: (low to the King) But, Sire, think of the scandal this adventure will cause. The poets will sing to you about it. Your enemies will rejoice, and the anecdote will make the Tour of Europe.

KING: (to himself) It's true. These English Puritans

will scream scandal, that court of Russia will be amused by it in its boorish leisure, and that Frederick of Prussia will add to his collection of nasty epigrams one about the Chevalier d'Éon. Well, we must shut their mouths. (aloud) Chevalier, come here.

POMPADOUR: (aside) What's he going to do?

KING: You've offended me and you deserve punishment.

D'ÉON: Yes, Sire.

KING: Well, if you wish, you won't go to the Bastille.

D'ÉON: If I wish—

KING: You are going to promise me to submit blindly to whatever I decide as to your fate.

D'ÉON: I swear it to you, Sire. And to the Marquise who doubtless has it in for me.

POMPADOUR: No, Chevalier, I don't have it in for you.

VOICES OUTSIDE: There he is, there he is. Over here, this way.

KING: Open that door and let's find out at last what this shouting means. (Enter Mignonet, Grecourt Saint Yves, Lauraguais, officers)

CHORUS: (singing)

Did you ever see such insolence!
Who is this bold fellow?
That in his dementia
Brings trouble to this place?

MIGNONET: I want my Nana. I've got to have my Nana.

KING: Who is this man? And what's he doing here?

SAINT YVES: Sire, although an outsider, they found him dressed in the livery of the château and furnished with a key to this pavillion. He brought trouble to the salons, looking at every lady in the most extravagant manner. We've had a thousand troubles arresting him.

KING: That's fine! Take him to the city jail and leave us.

POMPADOUR: A word in his favor, Sire. That young man is mad.

MIGNONET: What! I am crazy!

POMPADOUR: He imagines that a great lord, an august personnage intended to carry off his fiancé, the young Marie.

MIGNONET: Marie! Anna!

KING: (aside) What do I hear?

POMPADOUR: But as for me, I am positive the young girl is in Metz where she's awaiting her future husband.

MIGNONET: Then I am hoping to take the coach to Lorraine right away.

POMPADOUR: If the King wishes it.

KING: Yes, we wish it.

MIGNONET: (to Saint Yves) We wish it.

KING: (low) You knew everything, Marquise?

POMPADOUR: (low) I've forgotten everything.

KING: As for Mademoiselle—

SAINT YVES, GRECOURT AND THE OTHERS: (aside) Mademoiselle.

KING: Since the Marquise takes an interest in all the guilty parties, she's going to learn his fate. (to Officers) You must be surprised, gentlemen of the Royal Dragoons, to see under this dress one of the officers of your regiment.

SAINT YVES: (low) The King doesn't know anything.

MIGNONET: You are saying, sir— (Saint Yves pushes

him away.)

GRECOURT: (low) The King knows everything and we must know nothing.

KING: But this isn't the first scandal of this transvestitism, and we have to put a stop to such intrigues. Summoned before us, this person, up till now the object of a thousand rumors and absurd conjectures has confessed to us she is the Chevaliere d'Éon.

ALL: The Chevaliere d'Éon.

MISS BLANGY: She's a woman, ah.

KING: And on her freedom, she has sworn to us that henceforth she will only wear the habits of her sex. Is this true, Mademoiselle?

D'ÉON: Sire, I am incapable of contradicting Your Majesty (singing)

Sire, to your laws I am resigned.
Of your bounty I am worthy.
At last my secret is known
I'm a woman, it's admitted

(low to the King)

But if the English ever invade
Be sure, The King of France will find
The Captain of the Dragoons.

KING: Huh, Miss?

D'ÉON: (with a curtsy) The Captain of Dragoons.

KING: We order that this confession be made public and inscribed in our archives so that no one will doubt its authenticity, and that one day historians won't be misled.

GRECOURT: (aside) Ah, that's how history is written.

KING: Chevaliere d'Éon, we appoint you our envoy to the Empress Elizabeth of Russia and we charge you to negotiate the marriage of our cousin, The Prince de Conti.

D'ÉON: Ah, Sire—so grateful! (aside) Condemned to wear a woman's clothes! That could be useful to me in Russia.

KING: Tomorrow your letters of credit will be readied and the following day you will leave. Until then, you will not leave Trianon.

D'ÉON: (low) Madame, will I at least have my audience of dismissal?

POMPADOUR: (finger to her lips) Silence!

KING: Now, gentlemen, let the ball continue. I myself am going to set the example.

USHER: (announcing) The King's step.

KING: Marquise, your beautiful hand.

(The King gives his right hand to the Marquise; she hands a note with her other hand to d'Éon, which he opens and reads)

D'ÉON: Till tomorrow.

CHORUS: Do you hear the ball, etc.

CURTAIN

THE ADVANTAGES OF BEING UGLY

BY ERNEST LEGOUVÉ

CAST OF CHARACTERS

SUZANNE

MARTHA

THE ADVANTAGES OF BEING UGLY

The action takes place at the home of Villeneuve, father of Suzanne and brother of Martha.

SUZANNE: (entering and placing her hat on some furniture) I'm here!

MARTHA: At last! Come back for lunch at one!

SUZANNE: I had a lot to do. Three lessons to give this morning!

MARTHA: Where?

SUZANNE: First at Mrs. de Brignoles.

MARTHA: Oh! Then I understand your delay.

SUZANNE: Do you have it in for de Brignoles, auntie?

MARTHA: Me, not at all!

SUZANNE: She is so nice to me!

MARTHA: Oh! Very nice.

SUZANNE: And her daughter and her son, too!

MARTHA: Yes, the handsome Captain.

SUZANNE: Ah! what's the matter with you?

MARTHA: The matter, is, Suzanne that I don't like to see you running about all alone in this frightful Paris.

SUZANNE: That's the fate of girls who have nothing; I have to earn a living. As for you, didn't you do something?

MARTHA: Oh! me, that's quite different. First of all, I am greatly your senior and then, I have a talisman.

SUZANNE: A talisman!

MARTHA: My face.

SUZANNE: What do you mean?

MARTHA: Look me in the face.

SUZANNE: Well?

MARTHA: Well, I am ugly: there you have it!

SUZANNE: Ugly! you dare to say—

MARTHA: It's not me who says it. (pointing to her face) This does.

SUZANNE: You wouldn't speak so gaily if you believed that.

MARTHA: I speak gaily of it, because that's what enchants me.

SUZANNE: Oh, for goodness sake.

MARTHA: It's so useful. What's the finest part in life. It's to be a young bachelor. Well, an ugly girl is a bachelor. She does what she wants, she goes where she wants. If I were pretty, I could take our cousin by the arm and go for a stroll: they'd say immediately: "Ah! two lovebirds!" Whereas now, when they meet us, what do they say? "A brother and his sister!" An ugly girl is always a sister. But when she's pretty, how many inconveniences!

SUZANNE: I would never have believed it.

MARTHA: Let's understand each other: for a young miss, rich and engaged to a man like herself, beauty is only one more item in her dowry, but for a poor girl, with no husband, that poverty forces to adventure into the street, a pretty face is a peril at all moments. Well, my little Suzanne, you are too pretty to be poor.

SUZANNE: I am pretty—truly? Well, I'm quite

comfortable with that.

MARTHA: My sermon really works.

SUZANNE: Ah, indeed! but where then is this great peril?

MARTHA: It is—(after a silence) Suzanne, you were brought up in America.

SUZANNE: You know that quite well.

MARTHA: In that country, didn't they follow you in the street?

SUZANNE: The folks who go on the same side as me, yes.

MARTHA: Ah! It is impossible that some handsome young man, seeing you so pretty, didn't think of talking to you to tell you so.

SUZANNE: (bursting into laughter) Ah! what a notion!

MARTHA: What! They never declared it to you?

SUZANNE: Never!

MARTHA: Never in your outings, in your travels through New York, no man, seeing you alone, ever embarrassed you with an insulting proposal?

SUZANNE: A man to fail in respect for a woman! Why all the passers-by who have wives, daughters or sisters would instantly rush to punish him and defend them.

MARTHA: They'd all rush en mass like that? We must really profit from free trade to import these customs to France; it's true though that they wouldn't take.

SUZANNE: I still remember.

MARTHA: I was quite sure there was still something.

SUZANNE: It was a lecture on botany; we were only four or five women amongst three hundred persons.

MARTHA: And the rest, who were they?

SUZANNE: (laughing) Men! Is there any other gender but masculine and feminine?

MARTHA: You were in the midst of three hundred men?

SUZANNE: No question, because we were listening to the same lesson. Suddenly, while I was taking notes, I saw a little paper fall across my shoulder and onto my sleeve. It was folded in the shape of a letter.

MARTHA: A billet-doux!

SUZANNE: I thinks so, indeed.

MARTHA: French imports! And what did the Quakers say?

SUZANNE: There was a great murmur in the assembly.

MARTHA: And what did you do?

SUZANNE: As for me, I continued to write. Then, when the professor was finished, I raised my arm like this and blew the paper off as if it were a little insect! Everybody started to laugh, and to applaud. And the young man was forced to leave amidst hoots! There you have it.

MARTHA: That's charming! But it's not Parisian. In Paris, you see the reception given to pretty women—

SUZANNE: Why so formidable about it? Everybody greets me with open arms.

MARTHA: Precisely—with open arms! Folks are greeting you like that— ah! you won't fail to get it! In all of France there's an old fund of troubadours who— do that, so that when a man finds himself alone with a woman, who's pretty, poor and free—he has two thoughts: the first is to fix his tie and pass his hand over his hair; the second is to say to himself, "Ah, indeed, it's a question of paying court to that pretty lady over there."

SUZANNE: But I never return them! Who taught you

these secrets?

MARTHA: My talisman! Still the same! Because no one ever looks at an ugly woman, she has all the time to look at others. That's what I did and I saw. So, there you are Miss Suzanne Villeneuve, instructress, you are going to ask advice of an attorney, a doctor, a scientist; at your first visit he will pay you compliments; at the second, he will call you my pretty client; at the third, according to the date of his—birth, he'll slip you a billet-doux, take you by the waist or fall at your knees—men of the Empire still throw themselves at your knees, never quite getting back up.

SUZANNE: Yes—some old fools everybody laughs at.

MARTHA: Not at all! These are national traits! You go to solicit a minister, you find protectors, post scripts— At the end of two days the supernumeraries will shake your hands, the office chief will kiss you—on the face.

SUZANNE: What—he'll kiss me?

MARTHA: A bureau director! Do you think he'll be satisfied with the arrangements of his inferior? Then he'll escort you to the minister!

SUZANNE: What? Are the ministers also—?

MARTHA: Oh! No! no! That's quite different! The

ministers are quite above these petty weaknesses! Their function is still like a sacrament. They respect themselves! They respect you! And you have nothing to fear from them! But except for them, and the senators perhaps, all young or old, handsome or ugly, rich or poor, employed or living on their income, civilian or military, all troubadours! troubadours! troubadours! Troubadors and usurers, for they always loan by the week—at two hundred percent interest payable in—Not one who loves disinterestedly—not even a captain!

SUZANNE: (uneasy) A captain!

MARTHA: Well, yes! for, since the word is vile, it's necessary that I get to the point! Do you imagine that, if Mr. de Brignoles trudges slowly and frequently up our four floors, it's because he loves the sculpture on the wood? Mr. de Brignoles is in love with you!

SUZANNE: (smiling) I'm quite aware of that.

MARTHA: You know it?

SUZANNE: No question, since he told me.

MARTHA: And you?

SUZANNE: Me? I love him, too.

MARTHA: And you told him that, too?

SUZANNE: No question since he asked me.

MARTHA: (aside) She has responses that bowl you over! (aloud) Have you told your father?

SUZANNE: No, not yet! It's my secret. I have the right to remain silent! It's someone else's secret and I don't have the right to reveal it.

MARTHA: You haven't told your father about Mr. de Brignoles' love?

SUZANNE: There's nothing wrong in that! I will mention it when the time comes.

MARTHA: And when will the time come?

SUZANNE: When our marriage date is set.

MARTHA: (stupefied) Your marriage! You believe that Mr. de Brignoles intends to marry you.

SUZANNE: No doubt! Because he told me he loves me.

MARTHA: Huh? It's unheard of! What evidence do you have?

SUZANNE: When a man of heart says to a young girl: "I love you" and she replies to him: "I love you, too" it's over! they are married!

MARTHA: They are married! Ah, indeed! If everybody who said that was— Clearly, you are coming from another world! Ah, indeed! do things like that happen in America?

SUZANNE: It's all very simple; they speak to the Governor.

MARTHA: What's a governor?

SUZANNE: That's the name they give to fathers.

MARTHA: I like this name of governor well enough; it represents authority, discipline.

SUZANNE: Not at all. Not even fathers marry their daughters.

MARTHA: In that case who marries them?

SUZANNE: They do it themselves.

MARTHA: Themselves? Why, but in the end, this governor, you must still ask his consent?

SUZANNE: Oh, yes. Afterwards.

MARTHA: After what? After the marriage?

SUZANNE: (very simply) No, after the young girl has made her choice.

MARTHA: It's the young girl who chooses?

SUZANNE: That seems fair to me, since she engaged herself.

MARTHA: Yes! but it's the governor who gives the dowry.

SUZANNE: A dowry? Who's asking him for a dowry?

MARTHA: What, in America the young girls—?

SUZANNE: In America—the young girls are not forced to buy their husband; an honest man finds them all richly enough endowed, when they bring to the marriage an honest heart and a life without blemish. But here, I don't know how to prevent myself from blushing when I hear marriage spoken of. You'd think it was a market! Always this humiliating word. "How much has she got?" She's got—she's got what she is!

MARTHA: Dear child! So you believe that your poverty won't prevent Mr. de Brignoles—

SUZANNE: What's my poverty matter and what would be his plan if he didn't want to marry me?

MARTHA: His plan? His plan? And his mother?

SUZANNE: Oh! his mother, that's different! I am sure that this marriage is her sole desire.

MARTHA: Huh?

SUZANNE: She told me so in a thousand ways.

MARTHA: She told you?

SUZANNE: Not in words, if you mean, but in deeds. Why would she ceaselessly lure me to her home?

MARTHA: Why?

SUZANNE: Why does she constantly join me with her son?

MARTHA: Why?

SUZANNE: Why does she meddle in everything that interests him? Is it thus one can act with another woman unless she wants to call her her daughter? But what's wrong with you, Martha? What's the matter? Are you weeping.

MARTHA: Yes, I'm weeping! (kissing her) Oh! Suzanne, how you hurt me!

SUZANNE: Why, then tell me—

MARTHA: (forcefully, aside) No, it's impossible! No! I don't want to believe it. A woman! a mother! that would be too frightful! But for him, it's different—and my duty is to unmask him. To enlighten you. Suzanne, Mr. de Brignoles doesn't intend to marry you! Mr. de Brignoles will never marry you.

SUZANNE: Paul doesn't love me?

MARTHA: Oh! I am not saying he doesn't love you. I think, on the contrary that he's madly smitten with you.

SUZANNE: Well, in that case, what's he want to do with me?

MARTHA: What's he want to do with you! Oh! I cannot—I mustn't!— Just know that men are an abominable sex!

CURTAIN

COLIN AND COLETTE
by Pierre Beaumarchais

CAST OF CHARACTERS

THIBAUT

COLIN

MATHURINE

COLETTE

COLIN AND COLETTE

Colin is at the back picking flowers; Colette enters and watches him from a distance.

COLETTE: Colin, Colin, now where is he! Why, I see him amusing himself picking flowers. No question he intends them for me. Ah! how pleased I will be to receive them from his hand! But, what do I see? He's taking the trouble to make a bouquet, he's kissing it. Ah! Colin, Colin, how much I feel these naive proofs of your love.

COLIN: (running and hiding his bouquet) Hello, Colette. What's wrong with you? You seem upset to me.

COLETTE: Oh! It's nothing; but, what's wrong with you yourself? Your gaiety today surpasses that of all your other days.

COLIN: I've never felt so much joy.

COLETTE: Do you love me more than usual?

COLIN: Oh! That's not possible.

COLETTE: (laughing) Ha! ha! ha!

COLIN: What are you laughing about, Colette?

COLETTE: About your embarrassment.

COLIN: Eh! From what did that arise?

COLETTE: Come on, come on, stop constraining yourself. That bouquet you are hiding is doubtless intended for me. Are you expecting I will take it from you to offer it to me?

COLIN: What do you mean?

COLETTE: Come on, are you being childish?

COLIN: I'm not aware of it.

COLETTE: In that case, get it over with, Mr. Colin! Are you going to wait until I am no longer in the mood to accept it?

COLIN: Yes.

COLETTE: And where's that come from?

COLIN: Because it's not for you.

COLETTE: What do I hear? What! These flowers that

I saw you pick with so much care, this bouquet you took so much pleasure in making, that I saw you kiss with joy—

COLIN: It's not for you.

COLETTE: And you are refusing me it!

COLIN: Yes.

COLETTE: (excitedly) Go, ingrate! Don't ever show yourself to my eyes again. I am going to flee the places where I might meet you, and I abandon to my rival all the rights that I had over your heart.

COLIN: Ah! Colette, stop!

COLETTE: No, I don't want to hear it.

COLIN: It's only a frolic—

COLETTE: Leave me, perfidious one! You won't enjoy your triumph for long, and your tender Colette will soon know how to put an end to a life she cherished only for you.

(enter Thibaut.)

THIBAUT: Eh, by Jove! What's wrong with you, children? How you are quarrelling! You'd think you were already husband and wife. There you are, all in tears, Colette. Oh, Zounds! Mr. Colin, it's neither nice nor honest, you must have complacency for the beautiful sex.

COLIN: Eh! Uncle, don't judge me without hearing me. Colette is unaware—

COLETTE: (hotly) No, perfidious one, I'm not unaware of anything, and I am only too well instructed—

THIBAUT: (to Colette) Let him speak, Colette.

COLETTE: (hotly) I don't know how, I'm choking—

THIBAUT: You will have your turn.

COLETTE: (excitedly) How will he be able to justify his actions?

THIBAUT: We're going to see.

COLETTE: The ingrate! On the point of marrying me!

THIBAUT: (to Colin) What! So this is really serious?

COLIN: Will I finally be permitted to say a word?

COLETTE: (excitedly) What's he going to say?

THIBAUT: Let's see.

COLETTE: (hotly) Ah, what cheats men are!

COLIN: Allow me—

COLETTE: (excitedly) After so many oaths—

COLIN: To explain to you—

COLETTE: To always love me—

THIBAUT: (impatiently) Oh! Dame Colette, if you want me to know what it's about, then you must at least quiet down.

COLETTE: What! You are not yet at the point?

THIBAUT: And the way to get there?

COLETTE: (raging) I see plainly you are on his side.

THIBAUT: But—

COLETTE: (wildly) You won't do me justice!

THIBAUT: I—

COLETTE: The whole world is betraying me.

THIBAUT: (angrily) The plague choke me if—

MATHURINE: (running in) Eh, with what are you amusing yourselves there? The whole village is assembled to celebrate the birthday of the lord of the castle; they are all in a circle trying to agree on what they will do to divert him; some are preparing fireworks, others want to play comedies, the school master, who has the greatest wit, is composing songs, he's already torn up more than one ream of paper, he says he's not perplexed except for the rhyme, but our groom, Colas, who has neither rhyme nor reason, says that he wants to get to the point. What are you waiting for then, here, arms crossed, while all the world is busy?

THIBAUT: Do us more justice; I feel we're all animated with the same zeal, and if we don't distinguish ourselves, it won't be our fault. But it's a question of a little difference between our two lovers. You know how they loved each other yesterday. Well! They can't stand each other today.

MATHURINE: Eh! what's it from?

THIBAUT: Colette's going to explain it to you.

COLETTE: Colin refuses me his bouquet.

MATHURINE: Ah! Colin, that's not honest.

COLIN: Can't I commit a larceny for the lord of this castle?

COLETTE: (tenderly) What! It's for him you intended it?

COLIN: (in the same tone) And who else could steal it from Colette?

COLETTE: Ah! Colin, how many apologies I must make to you, but, at least, you will give me half of it? For I also intend to present him something.

COLIN: Beautiful Colette, as our two hearts are only one, this bouquet will be their image. And for what pleasure he takes to receive it, it will be you who presents it to him for both of us.

THIBAUT: And what characters will we appear to the rest of them? I have the same heart for him, as you know, and I pretend to be lying in the same bouquet.

MATHURINE: Yes, we have that in common with the whole village .

COLIN: We are really counting on it.

THIBAUT: In that case, children, since here we are all agreed, we are going to prepare our best to celebrate the birthday of the lord of this castle.

CURTAIN

CHASTE ISABELLE:
A PARADE
BY THOMAS GUEULLETTE

CAST OF CHARACTERS

LEANDRE

ISABELLE

CASSANDRE

VILLEBREQUIN

GILLES

CHASTE ISABELLE

GILLES: It seems to me, Master, there were big doings in your neighborhood last night. The old geezers played all night; yesterday evening they were a curious sight.

LEANDRE: All these splendors are causing me a sorrowful sorrow; for finally, Mr. Cassandre and Mr. Villebrequin are two characters who have means.

GILLES: By Jove, I think they have means.

LEANDRE: Finally, the two of them are amorous of my charming Isabelle.

GILLES: Yes, my word, these old fools smell fresh meat, they want it.

LEANDRE: If you are not going to assuage my misfortune, you can count that you won't have Mr. Leandre for your master any more.

GILLES: Oh well, what's to be done?

LEANDRE: Got to put them in a funk, make them

change their decision.

GILLES: Yes, we must separate them from this venereal fever which is torturing them.

LEANDRE: You put your nose on it exactly, that's where the prick is.

GILLES: I know quite well, too, where the prick is.

LEANDRE: Shut up! An honest man must never speak of his mistress.

GILLES: What I'm saying about her isn't to talk about her, but in the end a throat that's been cut and a deflowered girl, there's no remedy.

LEANDRE: That is true; but don't you know that there's always a way to rebuild a virgin, and that these old, old fogies are preventing me from getting in.

GILLES: By Jove, that girl there is less afraid of the entering than the leaving, that girl—there, she would like you always to stay in.

LEANDRE: You see quite well it's necessary to prevent these gentlemen from prowling around her,

GILLES: Oh,! in that case, our master, close your ass and open your ears.

LEANDRE: I consent to it, well?

GILLES: It's necessary for you to get rid of Mr. Cassandre and Mr. Villebrequin, right?

LEANDRE: No question. But how will you do it?

GILLES: By Jove, if necessary I will persuade them that an ass is a parakeet. Go, leave it to me to do, but I see Miz Isabelle coming.

LEANDRE: We mustn't tell her anything of our sham, she is so modest and natural.

GILLES: I will leave you two together, by Jove you've no need of me to tune yourselves up, meanwhile, I am going to take a good cleansing enema to my paunch.

(exit Gilles.)

ISABELLE: (entering) Ah, good day then, Leandre, why didn't you come to our place yesterday, as you usually do?

LEANDRE: Charming Isabelle, you were embarrassed, you had the old geezer, the curio.

ISABELLE: You know quite well there's always a place for you. You have something against me?

LEANDRE: Rather against God.

ISABELLE: (laughing) Ah, ah! and me, too.

LEANDRE: Charming Isabelle, you don't leave much to be desired. But Mr. Cassandre and Mr. Villebrequin are causing me pain, they ogle you; yet you do nothing to get out of it.

ISABELLE: That's what I was thinking on behalf of my dear lover.

LEANDRE: Gilles is preparing a sham.

ISABELLE: I will prepare a better one than he. My dear Leandre, let me do it. I see some one coming. Go away, withdraw.

LEANDRE: I've always done what you wanted. How lucky I am to love a person as honest as you, and who is up to snuff.

ISABELLE: Goodbye, my dear lover.

(exit Leandre, Enter Villebrequin.)

VILLEBREQUIN: I believe that there she is, this adorable Isabelle. Hello my beautiful lil' angel of Paradise.

ISABELLE: (taking him under chin) Your servant, Mr. Villebrequin.

VILLEBREQUIN: This girl ravishes me, she's modesty itself.

ISABELLE: Ah! Not at all, sir.

VILLEBREQUIN: Why, my beautiful child, I would really like you to come spend the day in my house, my wife's in the countryside.

ISABELLE: Sir, I never go to town.

VILLEBREQUIN: It's that I'm so afraid of catching cold; the colds are bad this year.

ISABELLE: If you'd like to come sup in my chamber I will have a salad.

VILLEBREQUIN: I'm all for that, my pretty.

ISABELLE: Isn't that better than spending your money the way you did yesterday?

VILLEBREQUIN: Yesterday, I made you see a curiosity, you will show me your little trick.

ISABELLE: You have only to speak. But, if you want to, you can loan me ten shillings to give you a supper.

VILLEBREQUIN: By Saint John, I didn't think of that; but ten shillings, that's a lot.

ISABELLE: Because I intend to make you a bargain, and after the meal comes the dance, moreover I have to pay my rent.

VILLEBREQUIN: Here, my pretty, I will eat less than a party.

ISABELLE: I will wait for you this evening at eight o'clock precisely; only knock at the door.

VILLEBREQUIN: Yes, my charmer, let me satisfy my impatience.

(exit Villebrequin.)

ISABELLE: (alone) Now there's one already fleeced and I intend to deserve the esteem of my dear Leandre, by getting rid of the other one. Good, I see he's coming here. (enter Cassandre) Hello my darling, my everything, I bet you were thinking of me.

CASSANDRE: You guessed it, my charmer. By the way, do you know I really wanted to dance very much myself yesterday, 'cause it cost me six sou for the hurdy-gurdy.

ISABELLE: I really believe it, but my dear Cassandre, I don't like to see you spend your money like that.

CASSANDRE: I don't like it much either; but you enchant me by speaking this speech, adorable little pretty-pretty, also I'll never do it again, but I wanted to divert you.

ISABELLE: It's not the blind that I love the best.

CASSANDRE: I believe it; let's go up to your place.

ISABELLE: Oh, for the moment I can't, but if you

want to come this evening at eight o'clock, I will give you supper.

CASSANDRE: You will give me supper? You are adorable, never have I known anything so charming as you.

ISABELLE: Ah! as for me, I love you, although I've never loved anything and I don't know what it is to do so.

CASSANDRE: So much the better, my darling, I will show it to you. How full of happiness I am!

ISABELLE: In that case I can wait for you this evening at eight o'clock precisely. When it tolls at the little Convent, just rap at the gate.

CASSANDRE: I'd sooner lose my life, than lose such a lucky piece of luck.

ISABELLE: You really love me so much then?

CASSANDRE: I'm dying of love; see how I'm coughing.

ISABELLE: So that I don't have to do anything? For in the end if you come to our place it won't be for nothing.

CASSANDRE: I'm really counting on that.

ISABELLE: If that's the case, I can beg you to do me

a pleasure.

CASSANDRE: Speak, pretty one, what can I do?

ISABELLE: My good friend, can you loan me thrity shillings?

CASSANDRE: But, do you know what thirty shillings are?

ISABELLE: Yes, my dear lover, it's because I know it that I am begging you to loan me them, I don't have enough to give you a supper.

CASSANDRE: As for me, I don't care to make a good buy; sobriety gives health, and health is the greatest of all goods. A salad, and let 'em love me, will satisfy me marvelously.

ISABELLE: Why, it's not so much for having supper; it's for having two chairs and a table.

CASSANDRE: We'll forego that; we'll eat on the bed.

ISABELLE: I have too much honor to receive you like that; I thought that you loved me; but you don't love me. I am very unhappy.

CASSANDRE: Well, my darling, I can't hold out any longer. Would you like fifteen?

ISABELLE: No, you don't love me. . . . . I am indeed

mistaken.

CASSANDRE: In good faith, I can't give you more — think of it carefully.

ISABELLE: (weeping) No, hoo, hoo —

CASSANDRE: I'm going; I can't see you in this affliction.

ISABELLE: Hoo, hoo, hoo—

CASSANDRE: (returning) Would you take eighteen?

ISABELLE: No, I am really unhappy.

CASSANDRE: Come on, you've got to be reasonable as well, and diminish something on your side; I will place twenty and that's all I can do.

ISABELLE: And as for me, in good conscience, I cannot. They love you and this is what happens.

CASSANDRE: Why, also thirty!

ISABELLE: I'm not worth it, right. Hoo, hoo!

CASSANDRE: You're worth all you can be worth. But thirty shillings!

ISABELLE: There's only one word that will do: either you want it or you don't want it.

CASSANDRE: Judge by the excess of my love. Here.

ISABELLE: Why that's only fifteen.

CASSANDRE: I will give you the rest after supper.

ISABELLE: That being the case, it can't be done. What! You have esteem for me, and you are not proud of your Isabelle?

CASSANDRE: Here's the other fifteen.

ISABELLE: (laughing) Till this evening when eight o'clock strikes. I await you. Knock at the gate, and be very careful to be noticed. How happy I am to have a lover like Mr. Cassandre.

CASSANDRE: Till tonight, my pretty, I'll be careful not to miss it. Thirty shillings. What love makes you do! Thirty shillings, thirty shillings!

(exit Cassandre.)

ISABELLE: (alone) And from the two of them! My dear lover will no longer reproach me with not knowing how to earn my bread. For we have wherewithal to do it. But isn't that him I see coming?

LEANDRE: (entering) Well, my charmer, what have you done?

ISABELLE: I've earned thirty shillings.

LEANDRE: Now that's what they call knowing how to live.

ISABELLE: It's for our supper.

LEANDRE: There has to be a little order in all that one does, and you go to work too fast, I've already told you that.

ISABELLE: That's true, I get a bit carried away, but I will correct myself; I am doing it for the best.

LEANDRE: You are a bit too well known in the neighborhood; you must move.

ISABELLE: I will do all that you like, my dear lover; I shall have soon changed residence you know.

LEANDRE: I'll take care of everything since you have cash.

ISABELLE: Willingly. I will leave the neighborhood very soon if you find it agreeable, for I've given a rendezvous at eight o'clock to these two old geezers, and I would much prefer for them to find me out of the nest.

LEANDRE: That wouldn't be honest; they must find you at home, but don't open.

ISABELLE: Ah! my dear lover, I really think they can never open; don't be uneasy for you are a bit jealous, and quite assuredly you are very wrong.

LEANDRE: I am going to disguise myself; let me do it and we will see a fine sport.

ISABELLE: Ah! my dear lover, don't kill them.

LEANDRE: As for me, I am not killing anybody; but I intend to avenge myself for the insolence they've had in making dishonest proposals to you.

ISABELLE: I am going back to our place, and I will await you with an expectant expectation.

(exit Isabelle.)

VILLEBREQUIN: (entering) Now's the hour or I am much deceived .

CASSANDRE: (entering) When will it be a little sooner, impatience always gives pleasure to beautiful; people. Let's rap!

BOTH AT THE SAME TIME: Who goes there? It is I, charming Isabelle. Who you?

CASSANDRE, VILLEBREQUIN: You? You? Yes, I — Me!

CASSANDRE: Go, you are an old fool.

VILLEBREQUIN: Here's a handsome amorous gallant

of seventy years.

CASSANDRE: That's not true; I'm only sixty-eight, come plum time. Aren't you older?

VILLEBREQUIN: I'm as old as I am, that's not your affair.

CASSANDRE: But what are you asking for at this gate?

VILLEBREQUIN: For that matter, what are you asking for?

CASSANDRE: I want you to get out of here.

VILLEBREQUIN: I'm not going, and I will kick you out.

CASSANDRE: You'll kick me out, old fool?

VILLEBREQUIN: We'll see about that, old run-down clock.

(enter LEANDRE AND GILLES dressed as an ARCHER, Police of the night watch.)

LEANDRE: What uproar is this that I hear down there?

CASSANDRE, VILLEBREQUIN: (at the same time) It's not me, it's this old fool. Sir, he's the one who is wrong. Sir, I will give you—

LEANDRE: Give it to me right away. (after having taken the money he says to GILLES) Sir, do your duty.

(Gilles leads them away.)

LEANDRE: (To Isabelle who is in her house) Come, miss, come down. We can now slave at our leisure, and enjoy the sweet fruit of our chaste loves.

GILLES: (releasing them in the wings) Go, gentlemen, make peace, believe me, I am going to drink to your health. Now that's what it is to dine abroad.

(Cassandre and Villebrequin are tied and bound face to face; they struggle, fall to the earth, and fight, soon up, soon down, and they go rolling out.)

CURTAIN

PREGNANT WITH VIRTUE
by Thomas Gueullette

CAST OF CHARACTERS

CASSANDRE

ISABELLE

GILLES

LEANDRE

THE DOCTOR

PREGNANT WITH VIRTUE

ISABELLE: Certainly, my dear Gilles, you are all my hope.

GILLES: Hey! now look who's being nice! The devil take you, Miss, for having imagined stratagems in the pro and con of your love, the turnspit of my wit is worn out; girls think they are always prepared, and with them, you always have to start over again.

ISABELLE: But what do you want to become of me? Virtuous as I am, must I see myself dragged into a marriage where from all necessity my spouse must be a cuckold. You know, and are not unaware, how I hate the doctor and how much I love Leandre.

GILLES: Yes, but sonofabitch you must reward folks when you want them to put themselves in mud for you.

ISABELLE: What reward do you want me to give you? You know I've not so much as a farthing.

GILLES: A girl has always a coin with which she can pay off her debts, and can coin this money in secret without fear of being hanged.

ISABELLE: What! being the servant of my father you dare? Surely, Gilles, that's a joke on your part.

GILLES: Oh, well do what you choose; for with your Doctor and your Leandre, with the plague which chokes them, I don't know how to set up your snares.

ISABELLE: I don't see how I'm to decide. Tell me, should I have myself carried off by Leandre? Should I declare my father senile? or instead should I poison the Doctor?

GILLES: Wait, I'll find a good way to prevent them from declaring, I mean proposing, the Doctor to you: you have only to declare you are pregnant.

ISABELLE: Pregnant! I'm not, my dear Gilles; how do you expect I could appear so?

GILLES: Eh, by Jove; last year you were, and you made it so you didn't look it, you can make it now as if you were.

ISABELLE: Shut up, you insolent. Know that I don't like words with double entendres.

GILLES: Hey, by Jove, it's not lacking respect to you, but I'm not going to be put out of countenance because it annoys you.

ISABELLE: Although your speech may be impertinent, I find it very useful. All right, I'm determined to pass for pregnant, that will assuredly disgust the Doctor, but mustn't we warn Leandre that it's only a pleasant trick I'm employing so as to possess him?

GILLES: You must really be stupid, Miss, not to see that if he knows the secret he won't make grimaces with a sufficiently good grace, and he won't come to the support of the game of fatherhood of our love stratagem.

Besides, as he is to be your husband, he must get used to the idea soon of thinking that his children are not his own.

ISABELLE: I am obliged to agree, Gilles, that nothing is so honest as all your arguments, and I submit to them without a backward glance henceforth. But for the swelling—tell me.

GILLES: Go, idiot, go, that's not a difficult thing to imagine! Withdraw, I see your father, I'm going to give him a story.

(exit ISABELLE.)

(enter CASSANDRE.)

CASSANDRE: Heugh! Heugh!—Heugh!—Ouah! Doctor! (spits) Doctor! (he sneezes) Doctor! (he blows his nose) He really makes you wait.

GILLES: Fever's got you, Mr. Cassandre, I don't know anyone so sick, so dead looking, so like a screech-owl as you.

CASSANDRE: What do you mean?

GILLES: You must have been born under a malign planet. Before you were in the pillory, you did two years in prison, your first wife gave you horns, your second made you a cuckold, you've got the face of a monkey, you look like a scorpion, you're stupid as a pig, your daughter last year was brought to deliver publicly, and here she is pregnant again today.

CASSANDRE: Pregnant!

GILLES: Yes, truly. I'm coming to prepare your mind for it—if you have any.

CASSANDRE: And do you know if it's a boy or a girl?

GILLES: Plague on the jade! Is that my concern?

CASSANDRE: And tell me by whom did she become pregnant? Is it by one of my friends?

GILLES: No, but it has the appearance of being one of hers. All your friends are old skeletons ready to fall in a ditch.

CASSANDRE: Is it my notary?

GILLES: Right! He can't impregnate any more.

CASSANDRE: Is it my solicitor?

GILLES: He can't produce any more.

CASSANDRE: Is it my attorney?

GILLES: He doesn't do settlements any more.

CASSANDRE: Is it my usher?

GILLES: He doesn't cultivate any more.

CASSANDRE: Is it my draper?

GILLES: He doesn't show off his wares any more.

CASSANDRE: Is it my tailor?

GILLES: He doesn't do that sort of needlework.

CASSANDRE: He doesn't do needlework, he doesn't produce, he doesn't impregnate any more. Here, scoundrel, take that for your negatives! (he beats him)

GILLES: Yes, oh! Mr. Cassandre, I am not ungrateful to such a degree. I am going, in a terrible way, to give it back to you in your belly.

CASSANDRE: What, wretch, you dare to strike your master whose bread you eat! ah—ah, ah, ah, ah.

GILLES: Yes, Mr. Cassandre, you needed that little adjustment.

(They fight and fall on the ground.)

GILLES: Now, there you are, on the ground, Mr. Cassandre.

CASSANDRE: Ah! I am completely out of joint.

GILLES: And me too. Do you need a little cudgeling?

CASSANDRE: What's that you say now, gallows bird?

GILLES: Wait, don't you have a nasty cold in your nose?

CASSANDRE: Yes, rogue, I've got a nasty nose cold.

GILLES: You need to keep it as warm as possible. Come closer, come closer. (he shows him his ass)

CASSANDRE: Get out of here, wretch, if you don't want me to slaughter you. But here comes my daughter, I have to reprimand her.

GILLES: And as for me, I'm going to go drink a pint and eat a slice of sirloin. Goodbye, Mr. Cassandre.

(exit GILLES.)

ISABELLE: (entering) Boo hoo, boo hoo, boo hoo, I can't stand it any more.

CASSANDRE: Show yourself, beautiful, show yourself. Eh, what's going on? You're pregnant again?

ISABELLE: (curtsying) Yes, father.

CASSANDRE: Why, these manners don't suit me: eh, what the devil, don't you know how to amuse yourself some other way?

ISABELLE: Father, it's impossible for me.

CASSANDRE: I don't say not to take a pastime once in a while.

ISABELLE: Ah! Don't pester me, I beg you.

CASSANDRE: But it's a question of proper conduct.

ISABELLE: It really is a question of wise behavior. It's a wise woman I have to deal with.

CASSANDRE: I don't know how the doctor will take the thing.

ISABELLE: He can take it any way he wants to.

CASSANDRE: Luckily, he's near-sighted.

ISABELLE: In that case he really might not notice it.

CASSANDRE: But, tell me, my sweet, whose child is it?

ISABELLE: Ah, father! you know how virtuous I am! Don't demand such a confession on my part; I'm afraid of accusing someone who might not be guilty.

CASSANDRE: I've always recognized good principles in you. But I notice the doctor.

GILLES: (entering playing horsey on the shoulders of the doctor) Hya! Hya! Giddyup! This man has a belly so stuffed with science that he cannot take a step; I had to lead him here myself.

CASSANDRE: Come closer, Lord Doctor, and come kiss my daughter.

DOCTOR: Willingly.

(The doctor has a very big belly. He collides with Isabelle who has a big belly and they bounce off each other and cannot hug.)

DOCTOR: Whew! Old Man Cassandre, they say that two mountains cannot meet, but it seems to me that's not always true.

CASSANDRE: Always proverbs! O clever man, clever man.

GILLES: Come on, now's the moment for the stratagem.

(Isabelle makes faces.)

DOCTOR: Yes, I am very clever, but—

CASSANDRE: Hey, well, today's the day you must marry my daughter.

DOCTOR: Yes, but—

CASSANDRE: She's got very sprightly eyes.

DOCTOR: Yes, but—

CASSANDRE: We are really going to divert ourselves at the wedding.

DOCTOR: Yes, but—

CASSANDRE: Yes. But—Yes. But! What's that mean? You know quite well that on these occasions one mustn't recoil.

DOCTOR: No, but—

CASSANDRE: All the preparations are made; the fruits have been ready for over a week.

DOCTOR: By all the devils, it's been more than eight months, so that the pear is ripe to fall.

CASSANDRE: What? Is it because you notice that my daughter is pregnant that you would like to break it off?

DOCTOR: No, but—

CASSANDRE: I'd really like to see you insult me like that.

DOCTOR: Listen. I made you a promise, your daughter made me a fat baby, let's back out.

CASSANDRE: Go, you are a moron.

DOCTOR: All vain, grasping, lousy, old pimp!

GILLES: Eh! stop I t! Here are two young kids who are going to cut each other's throats.

(Gilles pretending to separate them gives them blows with a whip . Everybody, including Isabelle, fights.)

GILLES: (shouting) Keep a look out! A cop! A midwife! I am pregnant!

CASSANDRE: Why, let's control ourselves, I notice Leandre.

GILLES: Silence, silence. (speaking in Latin) *Contecueses omnes.*

LEANDRE: (entering) No, by Jove, it won't be said

that I will be the Turkey, and I see plainly that there's no other role for me to take than to take my sword in my hand.

GILLES: Huh, what's this?

(The same racket starts over with the same shouts. Gilles overturns a keg of flour on the doctor, after which everyone bows to him.)

LEANDRE (To Isabelle) Don't doubt my respect, charming Isabelle, but what I am learning is very extraordinary. I leave Le Havre, where I assuredly spent several nice days, I come with fish and game wardens on my ass; as soon as I set foot on land, on to Paris, I got behind a coach, so as to arrive sooner; you know besides, my devotion is very inconvenient to me, and despite these obstacles which are sent me by the goddess Fortune, I learn as I arrive, that today is the day that must light the torches of your union with the doctor.

DOCTOR: Oh! I tell you—

GILLES: Peace.

GILLES: Shut up, codfish tail.

DOCTOR: I have—

GILLES: Shit up your nose.

ISABELLE:: My dear Leandre, your return has certainly much to charm me, you can be sure that you are the only one of my lovers with whom I wish to gamble on marriage, and I know quite well your penchant for staying so long in the provinces has only enflamed your love for me .

LEANDRE: Ah, let me embrace your knees, one hundred and one hundred times. But what's this I perceive?

ISABELLE: Don't be astonished: it's only a draft which slipped into the space between my bed and the wall, which caused me to swell up as you see.

LEANDRE: Miz, those are sorry excuses; think that it's ten months since I left for the coast, and that since that time I've neither seen nor fingered you.

ISABELLE: Well, I have to confess that it's a misfortune that's come to me, I don't know how.

LEANDRE: That's no big thing, charming Isabelle; I know the manners that a gentleman must have, and I regard you as my wife, there's nothing to prevent our marriage.

CASSANDRE: Ah, how ravished I am with the joy you cause me. Come, since the doctor no longer wishes to marry my daughter, I give her to you.

GILLES: Nice compliment! Ah! the swine!

DOCTOR: Willingly.

LEANDRE: But I take an oath on the hilt of my sword, and on the lock of hair you gave me when you granted me the favor at The Play in the Hay Tavern, of not sleeping between sheets until I have accomplished two things.

ISABELLE: What's that?

LEANDRE: First, charming Isabelle, is that since you are pregnant, your father will never die—except at my hand.

CASSANDRE: What do you mean?

LEANDRE: If you had put her in time in the Hospital, I would not ever have had the trouble I'm having today. The lamb is not guilty when it is eaten by the wolf. It's not the fault of the apricot when it is marked by the bites of unjust hornets, and when the child wants to go dew—dew, it's the fault of its mother if it ends up having diarrhea in its pants.

GILLES: That's reasonable.

DOCTOR: That's reasonable.

GILLES: (to Cassandre) Come on, prepare to buy the ranch.

CASSANDRE: (to Gilles) Rogue.

ISABELLE: (to Leandre) Ah, how you alarm me! And what is the other thing, my dear Leandre?

LEANDRE: Cruel Isabelle, it's to die myself, in person, before you right now.

ISABELLE: (weeping) Ha! (they all weep) Go, ingrate, go! I wasn't pregnant as you see.

LEANDRE: What are you saying?

ISABELLE: Here, perfidious one, that's all I have to say. (an earthenware pot falls from underneath Isabelle and breaks)

LEANDRE: Ah, what do I see? What luck! Too clever trick. Pot which gives me life as it perishes, fragments which deserve to be bordered with gold all around, don't doubt the esteem and the gratitude that I will have for you eternally.

GILLES: He really wants that pot, but as for me, I'd prefer a tureen of beef stew.

COUPLETS

CASSANDRE: Love, come down to help me,
Deign to listen to me.
Revive the youth
Of Mr. Nice-guy, Cassandre.

While marrying my daughter,
Don't refuse me,
Use your crutch
Like a spade.

GILLES: Pretty masculine maskers,
And beautiful female maskers,
Take pleasure without end;
Be ardently faithful:
If you believe Gilles,
You must, this Mardi–Gras,
Use your crutch
Like a spade.

CURTAIN

ABOUT THE AUTHOR

Frank J. Morlock has written and translated many plays since retiring from the legal profession in 1992. His translations have also appeared on Project Gutenberg, the Alexandre Dumas Père web page, Literature in the Age of Napoléon, Infinite Artistries.com, and Munsey's (formerly Blackmask). In 2006 he received an award from the North American Jules Verne Society for his translations of Verne's plays. He lives and works in México.

www.ingramcontent.com/pod-product-compliance
Lightning Source LLC
LaVergne TN
LVHW041626070426
835507LV00008B/471